A FRESH WORD
A 31 Day Devotional

Kenneth R. Walls

TBM Publishing

A Fresh Word

A 31 Day Devotional

Touched By Mercy Ministries

P.O Box 1303

Silverdale, Washington 98383

Other Books by Kenneth R. Walls:

Falling Off The Mountain

Climbing Again (Four essential step after a spiritual fall)

Please visit our website at www.touchedbymercyministries.com

Day 1: Pardoned

Testimonies of the Saving Grace of Jesus Christ; we all have one, if indeed we gave our life to Jesus. To some it is such a distant memory you can hardly remember when you were not saved. To others it is a more recent occurrence, and still to others perhaps, the decision has not yet been made. To the latter let me begin by saying today is your day. For **2 Corinthians 6:2b** says, *"…Behold, now is the accepted time; behold, now is the day of salvation."*

You may be asking, "Why are we focusing on what is seemingly the most basic of Biblical teachings?   Let me ask you this question. How often do you sit and reflect on where the Lord has brought you from? You see I believe that as we reflect it changes how we view others who have yet to come to Christ!

Jeremiah 33:1-11 says, [1] *"Moreover the word of the LORD came to Jeremiah a second time, while he was still shut up in the court of the prison, saying,* [2] *"Thus says the LORD who made it, the LORD who formed it to establish it (the LORD is His name):* [3] *'Call to Me, and I will answer you, and show you great and mighty things, which you do not know.'*

[4] *"For thus says the LORD, the God of Israel, concerning the houses of this city and the houses of the kings of Judah, which have been pulled down to fortify against the siege mounds and the sword:* *[5]* *'They come to fight with the Chaldeans, but only to fill their places with the dead bodies of men whom I will slay in My anger and My fury, all for whose wickedness I have hidden My face from this city.* *[6]* *Behold, I will bring it health and healing; I will heal them and reveal to them the abundance of peace and truth.* *[7]* *And I will cause the captives of Judah and the captives of Israel to return, and will rebuild those places as at the first.* *[8]* *I will cleanse them from all their iniquity by which they have sinned against Me, and I will* <u>*pardon*</u> *all their iniquities by which they have sinned and by which they have transgressed against Me.* *[9]* *Then it shall be to Me a name of joy, a praise, and an honor before all nations of the earth, who shall hear all the good that I do to them; they shall fear and tremble for all the goodness and all the prosperity that I provide for it.'*

[10] *"Thus says the LORD: 'Again there shall be heard in this place—of which you say, "It is desolate, without man and without beast"—in the cities of Judah, in the streets of Jerusalem that are desolate, without man and without inhabitant and without beast,* *[11]* *the voice of joy and the*

voice of gladness, the voice of the bridegroom and the voice of the bride, the voice of those who will say: "'Praise the LORD of hosts, for the LORD is good, for His mercy endures forever— and of those who will bring the sacrifice of praise into the house of the LORD. For I will cause the captives of the land to return as at the first,' says the LORD."

"Pardon!"

We generally hear this word spoken at the end of each four year term of the presidency

Article II, Section 2 of the constitution states, "The President ... shall have power to grant reprieves and pardons for offenses against the United States, except in cases of impeachment."

The dictionary defines Pardon this way: **to officially release from any, or any further, punishment somebody who has committed a crime or wrongdoing; to forgive somebody who has committed a crime or wrongdoing.**

Jeremiah 50:20 says, *"In those days and in that time," says the LORD, " The iniquity of Israel shall be sought, but there shall be none; And the sins of Judah, but they shall not be found; For I will <u>pardon </u>those whom I preserve."*

This is a huge contrast to what we believe in society to be a pardon.

A presidential pardon did not 'blot out guilt' or restore the offender to a state of innocence in the eye of the law. According to the law they were forgiven for their crime and released to society but they still had a record of their crime. Not so with the believers pardon- **It is blotted out, it cannot be found.**

The word pardon in Hebrew **is calach (saw-lakh)** meaning *"to forgive."* The truth is that God's forgiveness comes with an eraser—natural man's does not! We may say we forgive someone, but the memory of their sin, especially if it was committed to us sits in the back recesses of our mind.

I think the best example found in the word of natural man exercising godly pardon is found in the parable of the prodigal son. Now I know it is a picture of God's expectancy of us, but it also gives us an example to follow.

We know the story well, how one son desired to be on his own and do things his own way so he convinced his father to give him his inheritance early. His father released his son, with the inheritance, to go and try to make it on his own. But the son foolishly squandered away his portion on riotous living until he found himself wallowing around in a pigpen. Coming to his senses he desired to return to his father as a hired hand.

We pick up the story in **Luke 15:20-24,** *"But when he was still a great way off, his father saw him and had compassion, and ran and fell on his neck and kissed him. ²¹ And the son said to him, 'Father, I have sinned against heaven and in your sight, and am no longer worthy to be called your son.' ²² "But the father said to his servants, 'Bring out the* <u>best robe</u> *and put it on him, and put* <u>a ring</u> *on his hand and* <u>sandals</u> *on his feet. ²³ And bring the fatted calf here and kill it, and let us* <u>eat and be merry;</u> *²⁴ for this* <u>my son</u> *was dead and is alive again; he was lost and is found.' And they began to be merry."*

The father received his son back, not reflecting on his sin, but with forgiveness in his heart, welcomed him back in the same family position as when he left. He was his son after all. He didn't give him a secondary place, but a **new Robe, a ring, and sandals on his feet.** And then they had a party!

I have been doing a lot of thinking of how I perceive others who are walking in sin—

Do I see them as a sinner in **Need of a Savior?**

Do I see them as **Lost and needing help to find their way?**

Or do I just **see their sin?**

Can I see sinners as this father saw his son or as Jesus sees them? **Luke 13:34** says (Jesus Speaking*), "O Jerusalem, Jerusalem, the one who kills the prophets and stones those who are sent to her! How often I wanted to gather your children together,* *as a hen gathers her brood under her wings, but you were not willing!"*

Here are a couple more questions to ask ourselves:

Does my heart break when I see the fall of humanity or do I just pass it off?

Does my heart break when I recognize, in myself, my human frailty and spiritual struggles?

Psalm 25:11 says, *"For Your name's sake, O LORD, Pardon my iniquity, for it is great."*

A mother once approached Napoleon seeking a pardon for her son. The emperor replied that the young man had committed a certain offense twice and justice demanded death. "But I don't ask for justice," the mother explained. "I plead for mercy." "But your son does not deserve mercy," Napoleon replied. "Sir," the woman cried, "it would not be mercy if he deserved it, and mercy is all I ask for."

"Well, then," the emperor said, "I will have mercy." And he spared the woman's son.

Friend, you and I do not deserve the Mercy or Grace the Lord has bestowed upon us, but I am so glad he did! And the people we find it hard to love didn't deserve it either, but He gave it to them just the same.

Knowing that truth shouldn't we see the lost as Jesus sees them? Shouldn't our heart break as we look across our nation and see the depravity of mankind and cry out to our heavenly Father to save them; to ignite a light within us to dispel the darkness around us?

The apostle Paul said in **1 Corinthians 15:10a**, *"But by the grace of God I am what I am, and His grace toward me was not in vain;..."*

When you go about your day and see people pass by ask the Lord to help you see them through His eyes. And if you have never asked Jesus to become Lord of your life would you do that today. There is no better time than right now! **Psalm 103:12**, *"As far as the east is from the west, So far has He removed our transgressions from us."*

Question to ponder:

How have you felt the Lord's pardon in your life?

Additional Scriptural food: Isaiah 53:4-5; 1 Peter 2:18-25; Romans 9:33; Romans 10:10-12

Day 2: Approaching His Glory

Isaiah's ministry in the beginning of the book of the Bible which bears his name doesn't start out small in my estimation. He is thrust into this vision, wide in scope. He is shone the wickedness of Judah; how this once faithful city has become a spiritual harlot. Isaiah peers far into the future to the day of the Lord.

The immediate fulfillment of his prophecy was God's devastation of the Land of Israel through the armies of the Assyrians and Babylonians as His agents of wrath, found over in **Isaiah 39:6.** But in the larger prophetic perspective, the day of the Lord refers to the time when God will cast down all evil on the earth. Isaiah received from the Lord a glimpse into the far future.   All this is occurring even before Isaiah is officially called to be a prophet of God.

Isaiah 6:1-7 reads,

"In the year that King Uzziah died, I saw the Lord sitting on a throne, high and lifted up, and the train of His robe filled the temple.
Above it stood seraphim; each one had six wings: with two he covered his face,

with two he covered his feet, and with two he flew. And one cried to another and said: 'Holy, holy, holy is the Lord of hosts; the whole earth

is full of His glory!' And the posts of the door were shaken by the voice of him

who cried out, and the house was filled with smoke. So I said: 'Woe is me,

for I am undone! Because I am a man of unclean lips, and I dwell in the midst of

a people of unclean lips; for my eyes have seen the King, The Lord of Hosts.'

Then one of the seraphim flew to me, having in his hand a live coal which

*he had taken with the tongs from the alter. And he touched my mouth with it, and said: 'Behold, this has touched your lips; your iniquity is taken away,
and your sin purged.'"*

I have looked at this passage so many times over my adult life and have used chapters 6 and seven in my prayers, pleading that the Lord would, *"take the coal off of the alter place it on my lip for purification."* But recently as the Lord took me again to this passage I needed to wrap my head around what was really going on. What was truly happening to this newly commissioned prophet?

As we read this passage we can see the fear in Isaiah; trembling at the very fact he stood before the creator of the universe! He knew through the stories of Moses no one could see the face of God and live. Now here he stands right in front of Jehovah's throne. He must have been in awe at the very sights surrounding him; mesmerized at first by it all.   Then suddenly fear struck him, shaking violently and groping for something to hold onto. As the blood rushes from his face he thinks to himself, "what am I doing?!" and he then must have quickly turned his face away, afraid to look.

"I am undone!" he manages to squeak out.

What is the first thing that is happening to Isaiah as he stands near the glory of God?

He is made aware of his humanity! The knowledge that he was but a breath away from his life being taken encapsulated the young prophet. Then suddenly a seraph flew to him with a burning coal he had in a pair of tongs and touched his lips.

Now we as believers understand that the presence of this same God is with us, through His Holy Spirit, every time we gather in His name. But do you ever look at almighty God the way Isaiah did?   Are you ever reminded of your humanity and does it cause your knees to want to buckle. If not, why? I believe many have removed the sovereignty and fear of God as they approach His glory. We have half-heartedly come before Him in worship with no pre thought, no preparation.

As I was thinking about this study God reminded me of a passage I had read not long ago. In chapters 8 and 9 of Leviticus the preparations and instructions for Aaron and his sons to begin the priestly order were given. **Leviticus 9:6** says,

> *"Then Moses said, 'this is the thing which the Lord commanded*
>
> *you to do, and the glory of the Lord will appear to you.'"*

If the priests follow the preparation God had given He would appear to them!

Fast forward to chapter 10—after the sacrifice of worship to the Lord had ended two of Aarons boys get a wild hair. Look at what it says, *Leviticus 10:1-3,*

> *"Then Nadab and Abihu, the sons of Aaron, each took his censer and put fire in it, put incense on it, and offered profane fire before the Lord, which He had not commanded them. So fire went out from the Lord and devoured them, and they died before the Lord. And Moses said to Aaron, 'This is what the Lord spoke, saying', 'by those who come near Me I must be regarded as holy; and before all the people I must be glorified.' And Aaron held his peace."*

What went wrong there?

These two guys had the instructions. They had all the right tools, but their attitude was not right, nor was it done as the Spirit of God truly lead them. None of this act was done unto the Lord. They wondered in and tried to take charge by doing their own thing. It wasn't about God it was about them. Who knows what was going on in their head? A little farther down in that chapter God tells Aaron not to go into the tent intoxicated.

Perhaps these two had too much wine outside the tent and wanted to continue the party inside, playing around with the fire. Whatever the cause they **did not obey!**

How often do we come together in our fellowships and offer profane fire. Our heart isn't into it; we have forgotten God's sovereignty or even really why we are there. It has become simply a weekly routine.

You may say to yourself as you stand in church to worship from time to time, "I just don't feel like worshiping." The truth is none of us feels like it all the time. The cares of this world with its financial insecurities, employment demands, and our responsibility at home bring on a great deal of distraction which understandably make it difficult to focus. No wonder we find it hard to function in church outside of a ritualistic mentality. To place our eyes on someone other than ourselves seems nearly impossible in our own strength. In fact, we can't! That is why the writer of Hebrews puts it this way in **Hebrews 13:15,**

"Therefore by Him let us continually offer the sacrifice of praise to God,

that is, the fruit of our lips, giving thanks to His name."

When we approach God's throne in worship we need to Get out of ourselves and remember it is not about me it is about Christ!

Let me ask you this Question, "Do you want to see His glory? If the answer is yes, then **obey and get out of yourself!** Remember what the Lord said in **Leviticus 10:3**

"...By those who come near Me I must be regarded as holy;

and before all the people I must be glorified."

There is a preparation to coming into His presence. And we find it so simply written in **Psalm 100:4 –**

"Enter into His gates with thanksgiving, and into His courts with praise.

Be thankful to Him, and bless His name."

Our worship is our preparation to approaching the King of Glory. True worship is so pleasing to Him that He will hold out His golden scepter and beckon you to approach His throne!

True sacrificial worship breaks the chains of selfishness and drives us into a spiritual realm of submission. The problems we are dealing with may not be gone at that moment, but our repositioning has begun to help us hear the voice of the Father saying "I am here! Step into my glory—it is all going to be OK! May the Lords shekinah glory surround you as you are lost in your worship of the Father!

Question to ponder:

What steps can you take today to move closer to the throne of God?

Additional Scriptural food: Psalm 16:10-11; Psalm 91:1; Psalm 100:1-3; Acts 3:18-21

Day 3: The Voice of the Father

In **Genesis chapter 22** we read the account of Abraham and Isaac and how God put Abraham to the love test. Would he be willing to give up the most precious gift he had received as a man to prove his love for the Lord? In **verse 2** the Lord gives him the command,

> *"Take now your son, your only son Isaac, whom you love, and go to the land of Moriah, and offer him there as a burnt offering on one of the mountains of which I shall tell you."*

The amazing thing is that Abraham went without the knowledge of how this act would end—just trusting. He didn't know whether he would eventually come down off that mountain with his son or not. This General of the faith climbed that hill with the idea that he would have to follow through with the sacrifice of his son. But, a miracle transpired and the Lord, just before Abraham lowers the knife to slay his son, steps in. The rest of the story is recorded in **Genesis 22:15-18** which says,

> [15] *"Then the Angel of the LORD called to Abraham a second time out of heaven,* [16] *and said: "By Myself I have sworn, says the LORD, because you have done this thing, and have not withheld your son, your only son—* [17] *blessing I will bless you, and multiplying I will multiply your descendants as the stars of the heaven and as the sand which is on the seashore; and your descendants shall possess the gate of their enemies.* [18] *In your seed*

all the nations of the earth shall be blessed, because you have obeyed My voice."

There are so many directions we could go with this passage; the willingness to sacrifice his only Son or perhaps the faith that God may provide a sacrifice at the last minute and spare his son Isaac.

This story is rich in content. But I don't want us to proceed believing this was just a cavalier moment for Abraham—twittely de, twittely dumb I'm off to sacrifice my son.

Abraham was a father and he must have had fatherly emotions during that hike up the mountain. I don't believe he was stone faced. "O, Father this is a tough thing you are asking me to do", he possibly whispers, as a tear slides down his cheek. "Nevertheless at your word I will do it."

It was something about the Fathers voice that brought up from with inside of Him the resolve to go!

He knew his Fathers voice—

He knew that if God said it then everything would be OK, what ever happened.

Ask yourself; would I have the faith to step out like that?

I know if it is me, and the Lord ask me to do something out of my comfort zone. My brain becomes one big question mark. "Father, is that really you?"

Abraham knew the voice of the Lord and he responded. He spent so much time with the Father he just knew it.

My earthly father has been dead several years now, but I can still hear his voice rattling in my head with that southern drawl. If I heard it I would immediately stop, turn, and listen. My dad wasn't a very big man, but to me his voice was. It was distinctive. KENNY!!!! When I heard my name with that many exclamation points I had better respond instantly, because if I didn't there would be consequences.   If I had not listened to the voice of my father I could have stepped into harm's way or made a wrong choice spiraling me into a devastating outcome.

Jesus spoke of knowing His voice in **John 10:27** which says ***"My sheep hear My voice, and I know them, and they follow Me."*** There is something about the voice of dad, especially when we are afraid. We hear dad coming so everything becomes OK.   The anxieties begin to subside. The psalmist wrote in **Psalm 107:29,** ***"He calms the storm, so that its waves are still."***

Not only did Abraham hear the voice of His heavenly Father **He Listened to His Voice**—the truth is you can hear and not listen? Children do it all the time. But let's not just pick on children; adults do it often as well.

King Solomon wrote in Proverbs 19:27**,** *"Cease listening to instruction, my son, and you will stray from the words of knowledge."* **Cleaning out the cob webs in our spiritual ears so we can hear clearly our heavenly Fathers voice and opening His Words helps us to not only hear, but gain understanding and know what the Lord is saying. The Psalmist wrote in—**

Psalm 119:130, *"The entrance of Your words gives light; It gives understanding to the simple."*

Not only did Abraham listen to the Voice of his heavenly Father, **he obeyed his Father**.
Abraham didn't hem and haw trying to wiggle his way out of it. But rather, even though afraid of the possible outcome he obeyed. Walking into the unknown is the toughest part of the test. **Hebrews 11:8 says,**

"By faith Abraham obeyed when he was called to go out to the place which he would receive as an inheritance. And he went out, not knowing where he was going."

Not only did Abraham hear, listen, and obey, he trusted the Lord. When we have a good Father like our heavenly Father we know when He speaks we can trust Him. **Psalm 32:10** declares, *"Many sorrows shall be to the wicked; but he who trusts in the Lord, mercy shall surround him."*

The sight of that ram in the bush must have caused Abrahams heart to leap. I believe on that mountain, during the sacrifice there was a wonderful communion going on between two Fathers and a son. I also believe Isaac watched his dad intently on how he responded to the voice of God and it impacted his life and became the example he needed to walk out his own faith with the same intensity.

If you have children, or if you don't, think of those who are watching your example as a believer, reflect at this moment on this question "have I made an impact on my children or those around me as they have watched me walk out my faith in my heavenly Father? It is a sobering thought!

I look back and have to confess I could have done it so much better! But, as we realize our errors and repent our heavenly Father loves us so much--He heals and restores. It is called grace and mercy!

I want to know my heavenly Fathers voice more! How about you? I am in awe beyond words of the mercy and grace He has shown me. And truthfully the mercy and grace my children have shown me! Each day is filled with more grace and mercy, and more opportunities to hear the voice of the Lord. Continue to listen to the Voice of your heavenly Father!

Questions to ponder:

1. How has the Lord shown you mercy this week?

2. What has Christ said to you through His Word?

Additional Scriptural food: Psalm 81; John 8:42-44;

Day 4: The Unknown

If you are anything like me, especially in these uncertain economic times, the greatest fear you deal with is the fear of the unknown. "What if I lose my job or my business fails?" "What if I become ill and cannot provide for my family?" "I may lose my car or worse my house!" All these scenarios are very real in our society for sure and may seem like justifiable questions. But they all begin with "what if".

It is just like our precious commodities. Speculators speculate that something is going to happen in the market thus driving up the cost. It hasn't happened yet, but they believe that it will. Fear causes a presumptuous reaction and affects all who depend on these commodities, you and me—the consumer.

For several years I suffered from panic attacks. Whenever one of these attacks would come on a very real physical effect on the body would occur. My respiration and heart rate would rise along with my blood pressure. At times even my body would violently shake and I would become dizzy. It was a very frightening experience! But, nothing serious was actually happening to me. I wasn't dying, though I thought I was. What was happening was a fear of the unknown. I was actually afraid of being afraid. If I was upfront speaking to a congregation the question pounding in my head was, "What if I have a panic attack?" I was fretting about the possibilities before they ever came into being.

Jesus said himself in **Matthew 6:25-34,**

[25] *"Therefore I say to you, do not worry about your life, what you will eat or what you will drink; nor about your body, what you will put on. Is not life more than food and the body more than clothing?* [26] *Look at the birds of the air, for they neither sow nor reap nor gather into barns; yet your heavenly Father feeds them. Are you not of more value than they?* [27] *Which of you by worrying can add one cubit to his stature?* [28] *"So why do you worry about clothing? Consider the lilies of the field, how they grow: they neither toil nor spin;* [29] *and yet I say to you that even Solomon in all his glory was not arrayed like one of these.* [30] *Now if God so clothes the grass of the field, which today is, and tomorrow is thrown into the oven, will He not much more clothe you, O you of little faith?* [31] *"Therefore do not worry, saying, 'What shall we eat?' or 'What shall we drink?' or 'What shall we wear?'* [32] *For after all these things the Gentiles seek. For your heavenly Father knows that you need all these things.* [33] *But seek first the kingdom of God and His righteousness, and all these things shall be added to you.* [34] *Therefore do not worry about tomorrow, for tomorrow will worry about its own things. Sufficient for the day is its own trouble."*

Most of us are very familiar with this passage. We have heard it many times over the years pounded into our head from the pulpit. But when you are going through something insurmountable it is hard to wrap your head around it. All we can manage to squeak out is, "but God I've done this, I've done that! Why me God?"

Verse 33 helps us to turn those thoughts around. Instead of saying, "but God", it says, **"but seek..."** You see, when we are at the end of our rope and we do not know what to do; we feel like we are out of control—It is then we can release control into the Lords hands, because He knows what to do.

I posted on the wall of my office what has become my favorite verse of encouragement during these challenging days. **Psalm 121:1-8 says,**

" I will lift up my eyes to the hills --From whence comes my help? ² My help comes from the LORD, Who made heaven and earth. ³ He will not allow your foot to be moved; He who keeps you will not slumber. ⁴ Behold, He who keeps Israel shall neither slumber nor sleep. ⁵ The LORD is your keeper; the LORD is your shade at your right hand. ⁶ The sun shall not strike you by day, nor the moon by night. ⁷ The LORD shall preserve you from all evil; He shall preserve your soul. ⁸ The LORD shall preserve your going out and your coming in from this time forth, and even forevermore. "

I try to read this passage every morning as I begin my day. I have to believe what the Lord has said in His word is true and believe it in my heart. **Philippians 4:19** says,

"And my God shall supply all your need according to His riches in glory by

Christ Jesus. "

We must stand on these promises and believe in our heart that the Lord holds us in the palm of His hand. The more we seek Him the closer we come to his throne. The closer we are to His throne the more we hear Him, and the more we hear Him the easier it is to trust!

As a child did you ever stand at the edge of the pool watching all the other children splashing around having a great time? Inside you wanted so much to jump into that glistening aqua blue oasis. The only problem was you hadn't learned to swim yet. "What must it be like?" you ponder. You notice the joy upon the faces of those moving about the watery delight with such ease and freedom. They appeared unafraid of their surroundings. You on the other hand were extremely uneasy.

Then, in the distance you notice daddy in the pool. And better yet he notices you. If only he were closer. Your heart palpitates with excitement as he moves near to where you stand. Now just a few feet away dad calls to you and says, "Go ahead and jump—I've got you. You can trust me!"

Those words from your earthly father are so comforting you don't think twice. You jump, because if daddy says it is OK, it's OK! Our heavenly Father wants us to trust Him in the same way.

Jesus may ask us to jump into the unknown, but when we come down He will be there to catch us in His strong loving arms. It is true that we do not know what tomorrow holds, but we do know who holds tomorrow!

Questions to ponder:

What fears are keeping you from stepping into the unknown?

How has the Lord showed you He is near?

Additional Scriptural food: Psalm 27:1; Psalm 46:1-3

Day 5: Jesus is coming

"Jesus is coming!" These three words to most believers bring an instant smile to their face. This short sentence most often causes an urgency to erupt in the soul, and should motivate us to be about the *"…Father's business?"* Luke 2:49. But the question we need to ask ourselves is, "does it trigger that type of a response in me?"

As I contemplate this subject I try to remember the last time someone simply declared that truth to me in a general conversation. On the other hand when have I? Shouldn't this very event be foremost on the believers mind? It is one of our greatest motivators I would think. In fact the apostle Paul wrote in **1 Thessalonians 4:13-18,**

[13] "But I do not want you to be ignorant, brethren, concerning those who have fallen asleep, lest you sorrow as others who have no hope. [14] For if we believe that Jesus died and rose again, even so God will bring with Him those who sleep in Jesus . [15] For this we say to you by the word of the Lord, that we who are alive and remain until the coming of the Lord will by no means precede those who are asleep. [16] For the Lord Himself will descend from heaven with a shout, with the voice of an archangel, and with the trumpet of God. And the dead in Christ will rise first. [17] Then we who are alive and remain shall be caught up together with them in the clouds to meet the Lord in the air. And thus we shall always

be with the Lord. ¹⁸ Therefore comfort one another with these words."

Perhaps we have become apathetic in our call as believers. We are comfortable in our routine and thus these simple words do nothing to stir our emotions and cause revelry to occur spiritually. If we are not careful we fall into the mind set of **Matthew 24:45-51**,

⁴⁵ "Who then is a faithful and wise servant, whom his master made ruler over his household, to give them food in due season? ⁴⁶ Blessed is that servant whom his master, when he comes, will find so doing. ⁴⁷ Assuredly, I say to you that he will make him ruler over all his goods. ⁴⁸ <u>But if that evil servant says in his heart, 'My master is delaying his coming,'</u> ⁴⁹ and begins to beat his fellow servants, and to eat and drink with the drunkards, ⁵⁰ the master of that servant will come on a day when he is not looking for him and at an hour that he is not aware of, ⁵¹ and will cut him in two and appoint him his portion with the hypocrites. There shall be weeping and gnashing of teeth."

Verse 48 is what jumps out to me in this passage. Our apathy tells us we have been talking about this forever so what is the big deal, we've got time.

We find ourselves not wanting to be moved into a feeling of responsibility for reaching lost souls. A friend of mine spoke these words to me, "Ken, I'm not evangelistic I don't witness to others." The sad truth is that this is the mindset of much of the church today. "It's God's problem, the Holy Spirit will bring them in." It is true that Jesus spoke these words, *"No one can come to me unless the*

Father who sent me draws him, and I will raise him up at the last day" **John 6:44.** But we need to understand the whole of Scripture. Jesus also said to Peter and Andrew in **Matthew 4:18-20** *[18] "And Jesus, walking by the Sea of Galilee, saw two brothers, Simon called Peter, and Andrew his brother, casting a net into the sea; for they were fishermen. [19] Then He said to them, "Follow Me, and I will make you <u>fishers of men</u>." [20] They immediately left their nets and followed Him."*

Friend, the Lord stocks the lake, but we fish.

We need to come to a place of urgency. We as believers know the Lord is coming soon. It is not as was predicted by many modern day self-proclaimed prophets; for the Bible clearly tells us *"No one knows about that day or hour, not even the angels in heaven, nor the Son, but only the Father."* **Matthew 24:36** but Jesus told us we will know the signs of the times.

When we talk about the Lord's coming what does it do to you? Does it spark in you excitement and the need for a militant response? Is your heart filled with a compassion for those who are lost or even a heart to encourage your fellow believers to persevere in Christ? **Hebrews 10:24 says**, *"And let us consider how we may spur one another on toward love and good deeds."*

Perhaps the very thought of Christ' return brings anxiety because there is so much you just haven't given up for Him. The simple solution? Surrender, obey, and get back to the basics of our mission while we are on this earth.

I remember a time when I thought long and hard about a mission's statement; words that best described the direction we were taking in ministry, whether evangelistically or as a corporate church body.

It is good as a ministry to write down what best illustrates your approach as a Christian entity, but often times we can complicate our mission—when all we have to really do is follow the example of the greatest person who ever walked this earth, the Lord Jesus Christ.

Christ' mission statement is recorded in the Gospel of **Luke 19:10** *"for the Son of Man has come to seek and to save that which was lost."* This statement reveals a proactive approach to sharing our faith in Christ. It is not a stuck in the pew theology, but a get up and go theology.   To seek requires action—a purposeful action of going after something.

Let's rise up knowing the time of Christ return is near and lay apathy aside and get "busy about the Fathers business!" *BECAUSE JESUS IS COMING SOON!*

Question to ponder:

Who could I talk with about Christ today?

Additional Scriptural food: Romans 8:15-17; John 14:2-3

Day 6: Covenant of Purity

The other day I had the privilege of witnessing a father and his son sign a contract of purity. It was birthed in the heart of this dad to celebrate this event with a ceremony.

We worshiped together, along with our worship pastor, and broke bread in communion bringing our hearts together in unity as we four men prepared to each place our signature on the document in support of this young man's stance to remain pure.

This teenager's father asked me to share briefly on covenant. Now, I do not recall a time in my twenty plus years of ministry ever teaching on covenants. I've talked about the new covenant in short as communion was being served, but in response to his request I began to see what the Word had to say and the Lord revealed to me some awesome truths.

The Holy Spirit immediately took me to the first known covenant account in **Genesis 9:9-11**—

[9] "And as for Me, behold, I establish My covenant with you and with your descendants after you, [10] and with every living creature that is with you: the birds, the cattle, and every beast of the earth with you, of all that go out of the ark, every beast of the earth. [11] Thus I establish My covenant with you: Never again shall all flesh

be cut off by the waters of the flood; never again shall there be a
flood to destroy the earth."

The Lord said that He established the covenant. Established means, *to start or set up something that is intended to continue or* **_be permanent_**. God set in motion something that was binding and could not be broken, unlike a contract. Of course a contract is meant to be binding, but often there are ways of ending it. Sometimes there are consequences, such as, penalties and the ending of a business relationship. And then there is the fact that time has simply run out; whatever the reason it can come to an end because it is temporary.

When I have the opportunity to counsel a couple prior to the wedding I ask them this question, "Would you like a contract marriage or a covenant marriage?" I have yet to have a couple admit to me that they only want a contract marriage.

We always want the marriage to be permanent. For that to be the case in any relationship we must allow Jesus to establish the covenant inside. We don't just think on the covenant with our brain and thus it is established. The brain simply processes surface emotions. *Contracts come from without, but covenants come from within*.

Throughout the Word we see the establishment of a God ordained covenant. In **Genesis 15** God made a covenant with Abraham that his descendents would be as numerous as the stars in the sky. And they are. **Genesis 17:7** says,

7 "And I will establish My covenant between Me and you and your descendants after you in their generations, for an __everlasting covenant__, to be God to you and your descendants after you." And God told them in **verse 9**, *"….you will keep My covenant…."* We still see the reality of that covenant today.

Friends when God **establishes** a covenant He remembers it. Whenever a rainbow appears in the sky God remembers His covenant not to destroy the earth with a flood; **Genesis 9:13-15**,

13 "I set My rainbow in the cloud, and it shall be for the sign of the covenant between Me and the earth. 14 It shall be, when I bring a cloud over the earth, that the rainbow shall be seen in the cloud; 15 and __I will remember__ My covenant which is between Me and you and every living creature of all flesh; the waters shall never again become a flood to destroy all flesh."

And in **Exodus 2:24** Just before Moses was commissioned to bring the children of Israel out of bondage in Egypt it says, *24 "So God heard their groaning, __and God remembered__ His covenant with Abraham, with Isaac, and with Jacob".*

With this young man, as well as with you and me, God desires to establish not a contract, but a covenant of purity. He wants us to keep ourselves solely to Him in all that we do. **Philippians 4:8** gives this instruction,

8 "Finally, brethren, whatever things are true, whatever things are noble, whatever things are just, whatever things are pure, whatever

things are lovely, whatever things are of good report, if there is any virtue and if there is anything praiseworthy—<u>meditate on these things</u>".

But, let's not forget that the Lord did not simply leave us with the covenant of old. He gave us a new one through the death and resurrection of our Lord and Savior Jesus Christ! **Hebrews 13:20-21** declares,

[20] "Now may the God of peace who brought up our Lord Jesus from the dead, that great Shepherd of the sheep, through the blood of the <u>everlasting covenant</u>, [21] make you complete in every good work to do His will, working in you what is well pleasing in His sight, through Jesus Christ, to whom be glory forever and ever. Amen."

Question to ponder:

Do you remember the covenant of purity Christ has established within you; to be dedicated to Him and loyal? Or is it simply a contract in your mind to be ripped up and discarded when times get tough and the prodding of the enemy (Satan) becomes fierce?

Additional Scriptural food: Psalm 24:3-5; Matthew 5:8; 1 Timothy 4:12; Hebrews 10:19-25

Day 7: It's Test Time

It's test time! These three words alone have the power, when allowed, to evoke a myriad of physical and emotional responses. Responses like--increased respiration, heart palpitations, cold sweats, or even a far off stair (the lights on, but nobodies home). If your of the not so normal category, it could bring a positive response like elation (this response? not so often. It is a feeling one can only hope).

Let's face it, most people just do not like test, because we know it is there to measure our knowledge about a particular subject. We are afraid we may not pass the test and thus appear a failure according to the subject. What we forget is that each time a test is given it strengthens our understanding of the subject, if we learn from our mistakes, and it prepares us for future test that will come down the line along with preparation for a career we may enter later on.

This is how it is in the spiritual. The test we receive now strengthen us and prepare us for what will come down the line later; either a ministry opportunity, the resolve to endure, or a testament of Christ' hand in our life.

For curiosities sake I looked up test anxiety from a counseling centers web site. In their article were four points in bold lettering that could be powerfully used when dealing with spiritual testing.

The four points include:

Dealing with Anxiety

Preparation Can Help

Changing Your Attitude

Don't Forget the Basics

The question is, how can we turn these four points into biblical truths?

Let's see what the Word of God has to say about these.

1. **Dealing with anxiety**:

The first scripture that immediately comes to mind is found in **Philippians 4: 6**

"Be anxious for nothing, but in everything by prayer and supplication, with thanksgiving, let your requests be made known to God; 7 and the peace of God, which surpasses all understanding, will guard your hearts and minds through Christ Jesus."

Paul instructs the Philippians and us that we do not need to be anxious because we have a source to go to. And we do it right smack dab in the middle of our circumstance. But I think the key phrase in this passage is *"with thanksgiving"*. When we think the Lord before we even see the results an expectation begins to fill us and an incredible peace ensues.

Let's look at the second point;

2. <u>Preparation can help</u>:

How do we prepare for testing? If we want to have a shot at a solid outcome we must study the text book. It is our best source to help us understand what to expect. **2 Timothy 2:15** says,

"Study to shew thyself approved unto God, a workman that needeth not to be ashamed, rightly dividing the word of truth."

The New King James says, *"Be <u>diligent to present yourself</u> approved to God..."* We need to be diligent in reading and understanding, through the power of the Holy Spirit, the Word of God, which will prepare us for the tests and trials that come our way.

In Ephesians 5, a passage ministers use so often in wedding ceremonies, Paul is instructing husbands and wives in their relationship to each other, but he does it in reference to Christ' relationship with the church. As he speaks to the husband the apostle Paul says this in **Ephesians 5:25-27 *(NKJV),***

"Husbands, love your wives, just as Christ also loved the church and gave Himself for her, that He might sanctify and cleanse her with the washing of water by the word, that He might present her to Himself a glorious church, not having spot or wrinkle or any such thing, but that she should be holy and without blemish."

The Word of God cleanses our mind; keeps it clear from distractions helping us to focus on the task at hand-*"...being busy about my Father's business." Luke 2:49*

3. <u>Changing your attitude</u>:

I can think of no better place for an attitude check than **Matthew 5** where we are presented with the beginning of Christ' sermon on the Mount of Olives. In the beginning of this great message we are given a list of nine attributes or attitudes we are to walk in. As believers we have coined this list The Beatitudes. Here it is, as recorded in **Matthew 5:1-12**

1 "And seeing the multitudes, He went up on a mountain, and when He was seated His disciples came to Him. 2 Then He opened His mouth and taught them, saying:
3 "Blessed <u>are the poor in spirit</u>,
For theirs is the kingdom of heaven.
4 <u>Blessed are those who mourn</u>,
For they shall be comforted.

5 <u>Blessed are the meek</u>,
For they shall inherit the earth.
6 <u>Blessed are those who hunger and thirst for righteousness</u>,
For they shall be filled.
7 <u>Blessed are the merciful</u>,
For they shall obtain mercy.
8 <u>Blessed are the pure in heart</u>,
For they shall see God.
9 <u>Blessed are the peacemakers</u>,
For they shall be called sons of God.
10 <u>Blessed are those who are persecuted for righteousness'</u>
<u>sake</u>,
For theirs is the kingdom of heaven.

11 "<u>Blessed are you when they revile and persecute you, and say</u>
<u>all kinds of evil against you falsely for My sake</u>. 12 Rejoice and be
exceedingly glad, for great is your reward in heaven, for so they
persecuted the prophets who were before you."

We will notice after each of these attitudes is a promise
attached if we will genuinely walk in these traits.
Let's quickly highlight the promises:

V. 3 "...the Kingdom of Heaven."
V. 4 "...shall Be Comforted."
V.5 "...shall Inherit the Earth."
V.6 "...shall Be Filled."

V.7 *"...shall Obtain Mercy."*

V.8 *"...Shall See God."*

V.9 *"...shall Be called sons of God."*

V.10 *"..theirs is The Kingdom of Heaven."*

V.11 *"..Reward in Heaven."*

With a proper spiritual attitude the results are eternal; the benefits glorious and it will continue to spur us on to greater things, keeping us from falling into spiritual apathy which is unfortunately so pronounced in our churches today.

The final point which is so powerful is--

4. **Don't forget the basics**:

We as believers need to continually return to the basics of our faith. So often we try to over complicate and over spiritualize everything. I am continually reminded of Paul's words to Corinthians in **1 Corinthians 2:1-5,**

"And I, brethren, when I came to you, did not come with excellence of speech or of wisdom declaring to you the testimony[a] of God. For I determined not to know anything among you except Jesus Christ and Him crucified. I was with you in weakness, in fear, and in much trembling. And my speech and my preaching were not with persuasive words of human[b] wisdom, but in demonstration of the Spirit and of power, that your

faith should not be in the wisdom of men but in the power of God."

Friends our faith is all about Jesus, our life is all about Jesus and our walk needs to be all about Jesus; that in all we do or go through we endure it as unto the Lord.

Questions to ponder:

1. **Am I prepared for the test currently in my life, or those that are soon to come?**

2. **What must I do to be ready?**

Additional Scriptural food: James 1:2-3; 1 Corinthians 3:13

Day 8: "It is finished!"

These three simple words spoken over two thousand years ago still echo throughout the heavens. A phrase that set into motion a grace and mercy man had never fully known before, and still grapple with an understanding of its depth and width today.

For nearly eleven years I have journeyed back up a mountain I had stepped off of while following my own desires, a "fall from grace" we call it, but when I had traveled through the air shrouded in blackness I did not land in a black hole alone and forgotten, but rather I fell into the arms of grace once again. I didn't fall from it I fell into it. But where did it come from, and why? I didn't deserve it and I didn't expect it. But there it was, warm and inviting. Grace wasn't alone, but rather mercy accompanied grace; it's bright light of love surrounding it like the rings of Saturn.

Encapsulated in a love I had not realized I took that first step upward joined by my two new friends. Each took a hand and guided me over rock and crevice. As I would slip they would steady me and we would continue, so often having to repeat the process, but grace and mercy never left my side.

The climb has not been without pain and discomfort. There are loose rocks and boulders everywhere and hidden in the caves along the path are winged tormentors threatening to end the assent. But with each slip and fall the balm of Gilead is poured out upon the wound soothing each scrape and bruise.

As I pen these words, "it is finished" continues to flash through my mind; the finality, the completed work, all for me. In my spiritual eyes I can see Christ as the nails are pierced through His hands and feet. Writhing in pain He presses His head against the splintered timber, yelling into the darkness, "Father forgive him!" Then, "it is finished". What an amazing truth.

The daily reality is I have not reached the top of the mountain as I thought I had the day I stepped off. I will not reach the top until the day I enter into that great city whose *"...Builder and Maker is the Lord"* **(Hebrews 11:10)**

Until that great day I need to live as the Apostle Paul stated in **Philippians 3:12-14,** [12] *"Not that I have already attained, or am already perfected; but I press on, that I may lay hold of that for which Christ Jesus has also laid hold of me.* [13] *Brethren, I do not count myself to have apprehended; but one thing I do, forgetting those things which are behind and reaching forward to those things which are ahead,* [14] *I press toward the goal for the prize of the upward call of God in Christ Jesus."* **(NKJV)**

It's that pressing on that is so hard to wrap our head around. An elevator would be so much easier—so why the tough climb? What is with all the pot holes and jagged rocks? These same questions are uttered on a daily basis squeezed together in one manageable sentence—God why? But then what follows can even be more disturbing to our finite understanding—silence.

With the silence, if you're like me, come more questions. Why the silence? What do I do with the silence? Has the Lord forsaken me on this climb? Do any of these questions sound familiar?

The truth is these same questions, or concerns, have been tossed up into the heavens for thousands of years. Look at what the Psalmist wrote;

"O My God, I cry in the daytime, but You do not hear;
And in the night season, and am not silent." **Psalm 22:2**

"To You I will cry, O LORD my Rock:
do not be silent to me, lest, if You are silent to me,
I become like those who go down to the pit." **Psalm 28:1**

You and I sit in great company alongside those who yearn to hear the Lord's voice—to have Him quickly brush away the cobwebs of confusion. So why, in our understanding, is there so often a delay in the answer? Or is there?

In recent days I have come to see that in the silence comes an answer for that moment—albeit an answer we don't want to here. What is the answer? Wait!

Wait? This is the answer we least want to hear—yet without the wait we are not truly ready to respond to the rest of the answer.

Let's look at a familiar passage in Isaiah—

> *"But those who <u>wait</u> on the LORD*
> *Shall renew their strength;*
> *They shall mount up with wings like eagles,*
> *They shall run and not be weary,*
> *They shall walk and not faint."* **Isaiah 40:31**

We see in this passage why the wait is so vitally important. It brings with it a renewed strength; a lifting of our spirit that we might be able to continue on in the fight. The new orders are on their way for sure, but there must be a time of gathering strength and receiving healing. It is all part of the preparation. If we rush the waiting process will be weak and unprepared.

It is time for each of us to militantly press forward in our faith using what we have discovered along this, at times rugged climb, to be an example that we might *"...save some."* **1 Corinthians 9:22b**

Questions to ponder:

1. In what ways can I quite my spirit and wait on God?

2. What steps must I take to become more militant about my faith?

Additional Scriptural food: Psalm 25:5; Psalm 37:8-10; 2 Timothy 4:2; 1 Peter 3:14-16

Day 9: Why?

One Sunday after listening to a tremendous message on being "set apart from the world" preached by a friend of mine several questions began to flood my mind in reflecting that very truth.

All these questions begin with the word why:

1. Why, as believers, are we so quick to hurl insults and words of hate towards each other when the scripture emphatically says, *"Let no corrupt word proceed out of your mouth, but what is good for necessary edification, that it may impart grace to the hearers."* **Ephesians 4:29 NKJV**

Or how about this one in **Hebrews 10:24**,

"And let us consider one another in order to stir up love and good works," **(NKJV)**

Our mentality has increasingly become "all about me." We do not put others first and this is a Biblical mandate as well.

Is **1 Corinthians 13**, which we coin the love chapter, witnessed by the world through the life of the believer if we ourselves cannot put a gauge on our mouth and love as Christ' loves.

2. Why do we use the excuse that to reach the world we must be more like the world? Peter wrote in his first letter **1 Peter 2:9**, *"But ye are a chosen generation, a royal priesthood, an*

holy nation, a peculiar people; that ye should shew forth the praises of him who hath called you out of darkness into his marvelous light…" **(KJV)**

The word peculiar in the dictionary doesn't mean "the same as", but rather "unusual, strange, or unconventional; belonging exclusively to or identified distinctly with somebody or something." Shouldn't the world recognize that we exclusively belong to Christ? (Think about that)

A couple verses earlier in this letter the Apostle Peter declares in **Verse 7-8,** *"Therefore, to you who believe, He is precious; but to those who are disobedient, 'The stone which the builders rejected has become the chief cornerstone and a stone of stumbling and a rock of offense.' They stumble, being disobedient to the word, to which they also were appointed."* **(NKJV)**

We must be different; obsessed with the things of the Lord as it were. Let's let the world see who Christ is through us; how He has changed us.

I hear people say, when confronted on how we should respond to others, "Yah, but."

There is always a "Yah but." What if when Christ was told to go to the cross and that it was the only way said, "Yah, but" and didn't. I shudder to think where I'd be.

But Christ didn't do that! He said, "….nevertheless, not as I will, but as You will." Matthew 26:39b

Christ did so much for me yet I find it difficult to surrender it all. Why is that?

2 Corinthians 5:21 says, *"For He made Him who knew no sin to be sin for us, that we might become the righteousness of God in Him."*

I want to be more like Jesus. Will you stand with me friend and declare, "We want to be more like Jesus", and strive for that?

Jesus said Himself in Matthew 5:6 *"Blessed are those who hunger and thirst for righteousness, for they shall be filled".*

As I observe the state of the church today it appears that there is a lack of hunger. Why is that? I believe there is a spiritual cloud of lethargy that has enveloped many who sit in our pews today; keeping them from the pursuit that is involved in hungering and thirsting after righteousness.

Paul wrote to Timothy in **1 Timothy 6:11-12,** [11] *"But you, O man of God, flee these things and pursue righteousness, godliness, faith, love, patience, gentleness.* [12] *Fight the good fight of faith, lay hold on eternal life, to which you were also called and have confessed the good confession in the presence of many witnesses."*

We need to stand up and become more proactive in our faith; desiring to be nearer to the throne of grace, thus becoming greater reflections of Christ.

Remember, it is all about Jesus—everything we do is all about Jesus.

Questions to ponder:

1. **How can I be more like Jesus?**

2. **What have I not yet surrendered to Christ?**

Additional Scriptural food: Psalm 92:12-13; Hosea 14; Malachi 4:1-3; Ephesians 4:11-24

Day 10: Who am I really?

Who am I really? Have you ever asked yourself that question? I think in some way or another we all have. Some have a very high view of themselves and some have a pretty low opinion of who they are. Both of these thought processes are damaging.

The truth is we all have a commonality that unites us without even realizing it; a common trait we so easily forget. It's a reality that most of us as believers have allowed spiritual amnesia to block out that ultimately robs us of our effectiveness as Christ' servants.

Look at what the Apostle Paul wrote to the Romans in **Romans 3:1-20** out of The Message Bible—

1-2 "So what difference does it make who's a Jew and who isn't, who has been trained in God's ways and who hasn't? As it turns out, it makes a lot of difference—but not the difference so many have assumed.

2-6 First, there's the matter of being put in charge of writing down and caring for God's revelation, these Holy Scriptures. So, what if, in the course of doing that, some of those Jews abandoned their post? God didn't abandon them. Do you think their faithlessness cancels out his faithfulness? Not on your life! Depend on it: God keeps his word even when the whole world is lying through its teeth. Scripture says the same:

Your words stand fast and true; rejection doesn't faze you.

But if our wrongdoing only underlines and confirms God's right doing, shouldn't we be commended for helping out? Since our bad words don't even make a dent in his good words, isn't it wrong of God to back us to the wall and hold us to our word? These questions come up. The answer to such questions is no, a most emphatic No! How else would things ever get straightened out if God didn't do the straightening?

7-8 It's simply perverse to say, "If my lies serve to show off God's truth all the more gloriously, why blame me? I'm doing God a favor." Some people are actually trying to put such words in our mouths, claiming that we go around saying, "The more evil we do, the more good God does, so let's just do it!" That's pure slander, as I'm sure you'll agree.

We're All in the Same Sinking Boat

9-20 So where does that put us? Do we Jews get a better break than the others? Not really. Basically, all of us, whether insiders or outsiders, start out in identical conditions, which is to say that we all start out as sinners. Scripture leaves no doubt about it:

There's nobody living right, not even one,
   nobody who knows the score, nobody alert for God.
They've all taken the wrong turn;
   they've all wandered down blind alleys.
No one's living right;

I can't find a single one.

Their throats are gaping graves,

their tongues slick as mudslides.

Every word they speak is tinged with poison.

They open their mouths and pollute the air.

They race for the honor of sinner-of-the-year,

litter the land with heartbreak and ruin,

Don't know the first thing about living with others.

They never give God the time of day.

This makes it clear, doesn't it, that whatever is written in these Scriptures is not what God says about others but to us to whom these Scriptures were addressed in the first place! And it's clear enough, isn't it, that we're sinners, every one of us, in the same sinking boat with everybody else? Our involvement with God's revelation doesn't put us right with God. What it does is force us to face our complicity in everyone else's sin."

The truth is we have all been in the same condition as each person that is driving or walking by you right now. How does that very knowledge change our effectiveness in reaching the hurting and broken of our community?

It's called relate-ability.

Relate is defined as having a significant connection with or bearing on something. The word *Ability* simply means a natural tendency to do something successfully or well. When we put these two words together—we are able to *connect well!*

Paul understood his frailty and the slippery slope he could find himself on if it were not for Jesus. He wrote in **Romans 7:21-25**, *²¹ "I find then a law, that evil is present with me, the one who wills to do good.²² For I delight in the law of God according to the inward man. ²³ But I see another law in my members, warring against the law of my mind, and bringing me into captivity to the law of sin which is in my members. ²⁴ O wretched man that I am! Who will deliver me from this body of death? ²⁵ I thank God— through Jesus Christ our Lord!* **So then, with the mind I myself serve the law of God, but with the flesh the law of sin."**

Paul knew who he was and where he came from. He never lost sight of that. Paul also knew where he was going, and he set his sights on that truth. We see this in his many times before the religious leaders for persecution. He always shared his own story of redemption.

So who am I really?

1. I am a sinner who needed to be rescued—

    Psalm 40:2 (NKJV)

    "He also brought me up out of a horrible pit, Out of the miry clay, And set my feet upon a rock, And established my steps."

2. I am redeemed—

    Psalm 71:23 (NKJV)

    "My lips shall greatly rejoice when I sing to You, And my soul, which You have redeemed."

3. I am a Testimony—

1 Corinthians 1:4-6

The Message (MSG)

4-6 "Every time I think of you—and I think of you often!—I thank God for your lives of free and open access to God, given by Jesus. There's no end to what has happened in you—it's beyond speech, beyond knowledge. The evidence of Christ has been clearly verified in your lives."

4.   I am a child of God—

John 1:12 12

" But as many as received Him, to them He gave the right to become children of God, to those who believe in His name."

Now that we have established who we are let's remind ourselves **who The Lord is?**

1.   The Lord is Highly exalted

Philippians 2:9-11 (NKJV)

9 "Therefore God also has highly exalted Him (Christ) and given Him the name which is above every name, 10 that at the name of Jesus every knee should bow, of those in heaven, and of those on earth, and of those under the earth, 11 and that every tongue should confess that Jesus Christ is Lord, to the glory of God the Father."

2.   The Lord is Awesome

Psalm 29—

"Give unto the Lord, O you mighty ones, Give unto the Lord glory and strength. 2 Give unto the Lord the glory due to His name; Worship the Lord in the beauty of holiness. 3 The voice of the Lord is over the waters; The God of glory thunders; The Lord is over many waters. 4 The voice of the Lord is powerful; The voice of the Lord is full of majesty. 5 The voice of the Lord breaks the cedars, Yes, the Lord splinters the cedars of Lebanon.

6 He makes them also skip like a calf, Lebanon and Sirion like a young wild ox. 7 The voice of the Lord divides the flames of fire.

8 The voice of the Lord shakes the wilderness; The Lord shakes the Wilderness of Kadesh.

9 The voice of the Lord makes the deer give birth, And strips the forests bare; And in His temple everyone says, "Glory!"10 The Lord sat enthroned at the Flood,

And the Lord sits as King forever. 11 The Lord will give strength to His people; The Lord will bless His people with peace."

3. The Lord is Mighty

Psalm 24:7-9 (NKJV)

"Lift up your heads, O you gates! and be lifted up, you everlasting doors! And the King of glory shall come in. Who is this King of glory? The Lord strong and mighty, the Lord mighty in battle. Lift up your heads, O you gates! Lift up, you everlasting doors! And the King of glory shall come in."

Question to ponder:

How does my testimony relate to my friends, coworkers, and strangers crossing my path today?

Additional Scriptural food: Matthew 10:17-19; Exodus 3:13-15; 2 Corinthians 12:9-10

Day 11: True Worship

Josiah at eight years old had become king in Jerusalem. He was one of the youngest to ever ware the crown. Josiah, as young as he was in those days, was nothing likes his father Amon whom he was following in rule. While Josiah only desired to do what God desired, Amon did evil in the sight of God all his days to the point of worshiping idols. He forsook the Lord the Word tells us.

Being young, Josiah wasn't aware of all that was written in the law of the prophets though his heart longed to do right.

While Josiah was still a teen ager, eighteen, he sent his scribe Shaphan to the house of the Lord to have the priest count the money that was brought in, and then to distribute it to those who are repairing the house of the Lord.

At that time Hilkiah the high priest mentioned to Shaphan that he had found the book of the law of the Lord, and gave it to Shaphan. When Shaphan returned to the king he eagerly read the book aloud to King Josiah.

After hearing what was in the law Josiah tore his clothes, which is a sign of grief, because he knew his kingdom had not been obeying what was written by the Lord. In response King Josiah sent Hilkiah, his scribe, and several others, to Huldah the prophetess to inquire of the Lord. The Lord began to speak to them through the prophetess about all the calamity he was going to bring their way because of the disobedience of the people, but King Josiah would not see it because of how he mourned over the sin of the people, and how he inquired of the Lord.   Look at the words spoken by the Lord in—

2 Kings 22:19-20

"Because your heart was tender, and you humbled yourself before the Lord when you heard what I spoke against this place and against its inhabitants, that they would become a desolation and a curse, and you tore your clothes and wept before Me, I also have heard you," says the Lord. "Surely, therefore, I will gather you to your fathers, and you shall be gathered to your grave in peace; and your eyes shall not see all the calamity which I will bring on this place."

Now look at the next chapter, **2 Kings 23:1-25**, and see Josiah's response to what he discovered.

2 Kings 23:1-25

"Now the king sent them to gather all the elders of Judah and Jerusalem to him. 2 The king went up to the house of the Lord with all the men of Judah, and with him all the inhabitants of Jerusalem—the priests and the prophets and all the people, both small and great. And he read in their hearing all the words of the Book of the Covenant which had been found in the house of the Lord.

3 Then the king stood by a pillar and made a covenant before the Lord, to follow the Lord and to keep His commandments and His testimonies and His statutes, with all his heart and all his soul, to perform the words of this covenant that were written in this book. And all the people took a stand for the covenant. 4 And the king commanded Hilkiah the high priest, the priests of the second order, and the doorkeepers, to bring out of the temple of the Lord all the articles that were made for Baal, for Asherah, and for all the host of heaven; and he burned them outside Jerusalem in the fields of Kidron, and carried their ashes to Bethel. 5 Then he removed the idolatrous priests whom the kings of Judah had ordained to burn incense on the high places in the cities of Judah and in the places all around Jerusalem, and those who burned incense to Baal, to the sun, to the moon, to the constellations, and to all the host of heaven. 6 And he brought out the wooden image from the house of the Lord, to the Brook Kidron outside Jerusalem, burned it at the Brook Kidron and ground it to ashes, and threw its ashes on the graves of the common people. 7 Then he tore down the ritual booths of the perverted persons that were in the house of the Lord, where the women wove hangings for the wooden image. 8 And he brought all the priests from the cities of Judah, and defiled the high places where the priests had burned incense, from Geba to Beersheba; also he broke down the high places at the gates which were at the entrance of the Gate of Joshua the governor of the city, which were to the left of the city gate. 9 Nevertheless the priests of the high places did not come up to the altar of the Lord in Jerusalem, but they ate unleavened bread among their brethren.

10 And he defiled Topheth, which is in the Valley of the Son of Hinnom, that no man might make his son or his daughter pass through the fire to Molech. 11 Then he removed the horses that the kings of Judah had dedicated to the sun, at the entrance to the house of the Lord, by the chamber of Nathan-Melech, the officer who was in the court; and he burned the chariots of the sun with fire. 12 The altars that were on the roof, the upper chamber of Ahaz, which the kings of Judah had made, and the altars which Manasseh had made in the two courts of the house of the Lord, the king broke down and pulverized there, and threw their dust into the Brook Kidron. 13 Then the king defiled the high places that were east of Jerusalem, which were on the south of the Mount of Corruption, which Solomon king of Israel had built for Ashtoreth the abomination of the Sidonians, for Chemosh the abomination of the Moabites, and for Milcom the abomination of the people of Ammon. 14 And he broke in pieces the sacred pillars and cut down the wooden images, and filled their places with the bones of men.

15 Moreover the altar that was at Bethel, and the high place which Jeroboam the son of Nebat, who made Israel sin, had made, both that altar and the high place he broke down; and he burned the high place and crushed it to powder, and burned the wooden image.16 As Josiah turned, he saw the tombs that were there on the mountain. And he sent and took the bones out of the tombs and burned them on the altar, and defiled it according to the word of the Lord which the man of God proclaimed, who proclaimed these words. 17 Then he said, "What gravestone is this that I see?"

So the men of the city told him, "It is the tomb of the man of God who came from Judah and proclaimed these things which you have done against the altar of Bethel."

18 And he said, "Let him alone; let no one move his bones." So they let his bones alone, with the bones of the prophet who came from Samaria.

19 Now Josiah also took away all the shrines of the high places that were in the cities of Samaria, which the kings of Israel had made to provoke the Lord[g] to anger; and he did to them according to all the deeds he had done in Bethel. 20 He executed all the priests of the high places who were there, on the altars, and burned men's bones on them; and he returned to Jerusalem.

21 Then the king commanded all the people, saying, "Keep the Passover to the Lord your God, as it is written in this Book of the Covenant." 22 Such a Passover surely had never been held since the days of the judges who judged Israel, nor in all the days of the kings of Israel and the kings of Judah. 23 But in the eighteenth year of King Josiah this Passover was held before the Lord in Jerusalem. 24 Moreover Josiah put away those who consulted mediums and spiritists, the household gods and idols, all the abominations that were seen in the land of Judah and in Jerusalem, that he might perform the words of the law which were written in the book that Hilkiah the priest found in the house of the Lord. 25 Now before him there was no king like him, who turned to the Lord with all his heart, with all his soul, and with all his might, according to all the Law of Moses; nor after him did any arise like him.

As soon as Josiah discovered that things just were not right he set out to restore true worship to the one true God.

Earlier this week, when I read this passage in my devotions, I began to think about true worship and what that really looks like. Jesus in a conversation with, what the Jews of that day, would consider a controversial individual; one deemed less than, described the worship God expected in **John 4:22-24 (NKJV)**

"You worship what you do not know; we know what we worship, for salvation is of the Jews. 23 But the hour is coming, and now is, when the true worshipers will worship the Father in spirit and truth; for the Father is seeking such to worship Him. 24 God is Spirit, and those who worship Him must worship in spirit and truth."

The word the Lord Jesus uses in this passage for worship is the Greek word Proskuneo. It is an intimate word of adoring— kissing, as a dog might lick his masters' hand. And prostrating one's self.

Let's ask this question:

How does one get to that place?

I believe we can use the steps of Josiah as a model—

1. **Josiah humbled himself**

Isaiah 57:15 (NKJV) says,

"For thus says the High and Lofty One who inhabits eternity, whose name is Holy: "I dwell in the high and holy place, with him who has a contrite and humble spirit, to revive the spirit of the humble, and to revive the heart of the contrite ones."

And **James 4:10 (NKJV)** declares—

"Humble yourselves in the sight of the Lord, and He will lift you up."

2.   Josiah was broken and repentant

We just read in Isaiah where he used the word "contrite ones".

This word contrite in Hebrew is Daka (daw-kaw) meaning—to crumble or literally beat to pieces—crush, destroy.

Psalm 51:16-18 (NKJV) says,

16 "For You do not desire sacrifice, or else I would give it; you do not delight in burnt offering. 17 The sacrifices of God are a broken spirit, a broken and a contrite heart—These, O God, You will not despise."

3. He tore down the old

Josiah went to work removing everything that had been set up before the people to worship in place of God.

Other kings had taken down areas that were close by, but they would often leave the high places. Josiah went way beyond that. He took everything apart and even ground it to dust. The facts show that this young king didn't want to leave behind even the resemblance a reminder.

Paul tells us in **Galatians 5:24 (NKJV)**

"And those who are Christ's have crucified the flesh with its passions and desires."

And to the Romans he wrote,

Romans 8:5 (NKJV)

"For those who live according to the flesh set their minds on the things of the flesh, but those who live according to the Spirit, the things of the Spirit."

Questions to ponder:

1. **What are the idols in my life that I need to crush?**

2. **What steps must I take to establish an intimate form of worship to the Lord?**

Additional Scriptural food: Psalm 29:2; Psalm 95; Isaiah 66:1-2; Philippians 3

Day 12: The Making of a Spiritual Athlete

1 Corinthians 9:24-27

^{24} Do you not know that those who run in a race all <u>run</u>, but one receives the prize? <u>Run</u> in such a way that you may obtain it. ^{25} And everyone who competes for the prize is temperate in all things. Now they do it to obtain a perishable crown, but we for an imperishable crown. ^{26} Therefore I <u>run</u> thus: not with uncertainty. Thus I <u>fight</u>: not as one who beats the air. ^{27} But I <u>discipline</u> my body and bring it into subjection, lest, when I have preached to others, I myself should become disqualified.

Let me ask you this question—

What defines an Athlete?

The initial answer to that question that comes to mind for most of us might simply be "someone who plays sports." I played some sports, but had you watched me you would have never called me an athlete. You may have been amused and entertained by my antics, but in time you would have been demanding they place a real athlete to feel my position.

Look at how the dictionary defines athlete: *(somebody with the <u>abilities</u> to participate in physical exercise, especially in competitive games and races.)* The key word in this definition is

---

abilities. A true athlete has worked hard to develop the abilities to play and stay in the game.

Some individual's we might say, because of the generational genes they were born with, had natural athletic abilities and others simply had to work extremely hard to develop the abilities, but the truth is they both had to work hard if they truly were going to compete.

Paul's athletic metaphor he uses in the passage helps us understand the work involved in becoming a <u>spiritual athlete</u>. It is all about the training we put ourselves through.

So what makes up Spiritual Athletes that become victors for the cause of Christ?

The Apostle Paul started out this passage with the word <u>Run</u>!

1. There has to be Forward movement (Progress)

If we are going to condition ourselves and make ready for the competition ahead of us we have to start by getting our muscles moving. What better way than to jog or run. We start out slow at first, and then in time we pick up the pace.

Paul went on to say in his letter to the church at Corinth, ***"Run in such a way"***

There is a right way to run if you want to win!

Galatians 5:6-8 (NKJV) says,

⁶ "For in Christ Jesus neither circumcision nor uncircumcision avails anything, but faith working through love. ⁷ You ran well. Who hindered you from obeying the truth? ⁸ This persuasion does not come from Him who calls you."

The Galatians were starting out their run well, but were being side tracked by the bondage of the law and not focusing on the love that fulfilled the law. They were taking their eyes off of Christ alone for their strength in the run.

If a runner takes his eyes and thoughts off the goal and focuses on all his surroundings; the sights, the sounds, he will become distracted and hindered and possibly even stumble in his pursuit of the prize.

As believers we keep our eyes on the prize which is Christ Jesus, and relying on His strength to help us in running with endurance. Look at what the psalmist wrote—

Psalm 18:29 (NKJV)

"For by You I can run against a troop, by my God I can leap over a wall."

And

Proverbs 4:11-13 (NKJV)

¹¹ "I have taught you in the way of wisdom; I have led you in right paths.
¹² When you walk, your steps will not be hindered, And when you

run, you will not stumble. [13] Take firm hold of instruction, do not let go; Keep her, for she is your life."

2. Fight

The second thing Paul shows us in his writing is that he doesn't just shadow box—he fights with purpose. Paul goes through a training regimen.

He learns his weaponry and becomes very familiar with them. Look at what Paul wrote in—

2 Corinthians 10:3-6

[3] *"For though we walk in the flesh, we do not war according to the flesh. [4] For the weapons of our warfare are not carnal but mighty in God for pulling down strongholds,[5] casting down arguments and every high thing that exalts itself against the knowledge of God, bringing every thought into captivity to the obedience of Christ, [6] and being ready to punish all disobedience when your obedience is fulfilled."*

[10] *Finally, my brethren, be strong in the Lord and in the power of His might.[11] Put on the whole armor of God, that you may be able to stand against the wiles of the devil. [12] For we do not wrestle against flesh and blood, but against principalities, against powers, against the rulers of the darkness of this age,[c] against spiritual hosts of wickedness in the heavenly places.[13] Therefore*

take up the whole armor of God, that you may be able to withstand in the evil day, and having done all, to stand.

[14] Stand therefore, having girded your waist with truth, having put on the breastplate of righteousness, [15] and having shod your feet with the preparation of the gospel of peace;[16] above all, taking the shield of faith with which you will be able to quench all the fiery darts of the wicked one. [17] And take the helmet of salvation, and the sword of the Spirit, which is the word of God; [18] praying always with all prayer and supplication in the Spirit, being watchful to this end with all perseverance and supplication for all the saints."

Paul even emphasized the fight to his protégé Timothy—

2 Timothy 4:7(NKJV)

[7] "I have fought the good fight, I have finished the race, I have kept the faith."

The third aspect of our training as spiritual athletes the Apostle Paul clarifies to us is the importance for Discipline—

3. Discipline

Colossians 3:12-17 says,

[12] "Therefore, as the elect of God, holy and beloved, put on tender mercies, kindness, humility, meekness, longsuffering; [13] bearing with one another, and forgiving one another, if anyone has a complaint against another; even as Christ forgave you, so you also must do. [14] But above all these things put on love, which is the

bond of perfection. [15] And let the peace of God rule in your hearts, to which also you were called in one body; and be thankful. [16] Let the word of Christ dwell in you richly in all wisdom, teaching and admonishing one another in psalms and hymns and spiritual songs, singing with grace in your hearts to the Lord. [17] And whatever you do in word or deed, do all in the name of the Lord Jesus, giving thanks to God the Father through Him."

This passage deals with our character as believers in Christ. Developing a Christ-like character is essential to maintaining discipline and seeing ultimate success in our development as spiritual athletes.

Questions to ponder:

1. **How is my character in this fight? Is my head in the game?**

2. **What do I need to do to better discipline myself spiritually?**

Addition Scriptural food: Isaiah 26:3; Romans 12:1-2; Hebrews 12:1-2

Day 13: An urgent knocking

Just following Christmas day of 2011, after the last shred of wrapping paper was discarded, the shoes were kicked off and a delight that the business was over, I anticipated and he approaching New Year and all that might come with it.

What was different about the expectancy I felt with the close of one year and the dawning of the next? Each and every year I move into the next with the belief that this year will be better; something special is on the horizon—new challenges and opportunities, and there were. There are always new things, for we serve a creator God who has never stopped creating new opportunities; new moments to witness the awesome splendor of His majesty.

So what about that year? What was so special about it? First, I believe it was the beginning of something that is still percolating in my heart today; a stirring deep inside; calling for spiritual a preparation like never before.

During that period for two days in a row I felt a prompting of the Lord to get out of bed and pray. I tried to ignore this pulling and simply remain in bed and pray (it was 4:30am after all), knowing full well that I would get a few sentences into it and sleep would find me again. But, this time the pulling continued and I had no choice but to swing my legs out of my warm cocoon.

In my living room it wasn't long before I found myself on my knees crying out in response to whatever the Lord laid on my heart—usually beginning with my children. Other names would follow until I felt a release from the pulling that had leaded me to my knees.

The next night as I slept I heard an urgent pounding at the door—pound, pound, pound, pound! I stirred, but stayed put. A moment later I heard again pound, pound, pound, and pound. I sat up, looked over at my wife Kim, and she was still sleeping. I knew that had this been an external noise in my home she would have bolted awake. My wife has an internal intrusion alarm. Nothing gets by her. She didn't budge.

At that moment I just knew this sudden sound I heard was a spiritual internal knocking. The Lord was waking me up— urgently. Stared into the darkness I said, "Lord, what do you want me to do? Who am I to pray for? The same draw to get out of bed occurred. There was no battle to stay in bed on my part this time for I knew something was happening! I didn't know what or to whom, and perhaps I never would, but the one thing I knew for certain was that *if required a response.* I also knew this was not something a natural event; something was going on in the spirit realm.

I immediately went into the living room, plopped down in my recliner and began to pray as the Lord brought things to my mind. Again it began with my children and to the rest of my family—to my church and my organization Touched by Mercy Ministries and those involved in those ministries.

It wasn't as if a major catastrophic event in the natural was happening right then. There was no heart attack or stroke; no car accident or marital decline. There was a spiritual battle going on in the spirit realm; for the souls of my kids, for the effectiveness of the church. Satan and his minions were waging a battle to bring distraction from what God desires to do; the victories the Lord has wrought for the believer; to cause us to recoil instead of fight as the day of Christ return nears.

I have become keenly aware that as we move into a new dawn we must be ever more militant in our faith remembering the words of **Ephesians 6:12**, *"For we do not wrestle against flesh and blood, but against principalities, against powers, against the rulers of the darkness of this age, against spiritual hosts of wickedness in the heavenly places."*

Our time is short friends and we must be busy about the Fathers business, beginning on our knees for our loved ones and friends that they might turn their hearts toward Almighty God in this last hour, because I do believe we are in the last hour.

Many individuals are motivated more by being under the gun. When the clock is ticking and the deadline is fast approaching they suddenly shift into high gear and find their stride. If this is you then I have good news for you, we are at the eleven o'clock hour and the clock is soon to strike midnight.

To some of you the shortness of the hour brings much anxiety because you feel you have much ground to make up or you feel that your own spiritual condition is not where it should be.

If your heart is not right friend I plead with you take that moment right now to turn from your sin and give everything over to Christ—Please! You may not have very many moments left!

The Apostle Paul wrote in **2 Corinthians 6:2b,** *"I tell you, now is the time of God's favor, now is the day of salvation."*

Start today right with militant prayer and a heart and passion for the lost that they might find Christ, or if you are one that has struggle with your relationship with Christ make it right today! Do not get in the trap of self-affliction continually knocking you down and being held in the mire.

Let me end with the words of Paul in **Romans 10:8-10,** (NKJV)

"But what does it say? "The word is near you, in your mouth and in your heart" (that is, the word of faith which we preach): ^{9} that if you confess with your mouth the Lord Jesus and believe in your heart that God has raised Him from the dead, you will be saved. ^{10} For with the heart one believes unto righteousness, and with the mouth confession is made unto salvation."

Questions to ponder:

1. Is my heart right with Christ?

2. What urgent matters is the Lord bringing to my attention?

   Additional Scriptural food: 1 Timothy 1:14-16; 2 Timothy 2:14-16

Day 14: Right at the door

"Right at the door"—four words straight from the mouth of Jesus; words given in Mark chapter 13 to His follower to evoke a sense of awareness at the nearness of the Lord's coming.
He put before them the truth of what lay ahead; wars, rumors of war, earthquakes, and famines *"these are the beginning of birth pains"*, He said in **Mark 13:8b**.

Jesus spoke, farther down in **Mark 13:28-29**, *"Now learn this lesson from the fig tree: As soon as its twigs get tender and its leaves come out, you know that summer is near. Even so, when you see these things happening, you know that it is near, right at the door"*. Through these words we can see how Jesus wanted them and wants us to pay attention to what is going on. But, what do we do with that knowing? Do we simply sit and wait for that great day of redemption? Jesus told us to look for it in **Luke 21:28** *"Now when these things begin to happen, look up and lift up your heads, because your redemption draws near."*

If we are honest with ourselves I think we would discover that we get so weary at times that we are simply content to look up and sit while waiting. I mean we are ready, aren't we, to live in peace and harmony with our Lord?   But, what about that which is outside my little bubble? What about the masses who walk in darkness; those whose eyes are veiled? They look out, but see no hope. What about the hurting and down trodden? They believe there is a God, but they struggle to see Him revealed. What part do we play as believers in bringing about that revelation to them?

One morning as I sat in my home office following my daily routine of reading e-mail and facebook post I read my wife Kim's latest blog. You can read it at—www.kimberlywalls.blogspot.com (read post 79). In this post she began to describe an encounter she had with a homeless man at a feed a church we were attending was putting on. As Kim began to ask him how he was doing his response was gripping. Conviction invaded me as I read. I was reminded how I complained that my feet were cold and hurting the night before, while he fought to simply stay alive in the snow storm we had just gone through.

The question spoken loudly in my spirit that morning was— what is important? Is it sitting and waiting for my reward in the warmth and comfort of my home, or to remember the mission of Christ—*"to seek and to save that which was lost"* **Luke 19:10**, or as **James 1:27** teaches us *"Pure and undefiled religion before God and the Father is this: to visit orphans and widows in their trouble, and to keep oneself unspotted from the world."*

I know I do not stand alone with these questions swirling about in my head. Many of you reading this right now experience the same tugging in your heart; the same knowing in your spirit. But, we need to go beyond the knowing to the doing.

It is all about the mission. Let me reiterate Christ' mission out of **Luke 19:10**, *"to seek and to save that which was lost."* The

Lord's mission didn't involve just sitting around waiting for something to happen. It was all wrapped around being proactive—going after the unbeliever—seizing the moment.

Just prior to Jesus ascension to the "right hand of the Father" he gave us a mandate to follow as believers. We find this in **Mark 16:15** (NKJV)

"And He said to them, "Go into all the world and preach the gospel to every creature."

Christ began His statement with an action word, *"Go"*. Again, the directive was not for us to stand still, but to move—find those who are hurting and broken and show them a new and lasting way.

The day is coming very soon friends when we will see the Lord coming in the clouds of glory for His bride, but until that day let's get busy showing the Love of Jesus Christ to a lost and dying world; showing them that though this world is full of trouble and heart ache there is hope in Jesus.

Question to ponder:

1. Who can I seek for Christ?

2. How bright is my light for Christ?

Additional Scriptural food: Galatians 6:15; Ephesians 4:17-24

Day 15: Standing tall in the midst of adversity

Why is this happening to me? Am I being punished? I wish I had never been born! These are familiar words many of us have uttered, or at least thought during a crisis. We hesitate to admit, especially as a Christian, these thoughts of despair would swirl around our mind. They surly couldn't be normal for a person who professes his trust in Christ, right?

As I sit and ponder this question this I am reminded of the human nature of man even evidenced in the lives of those whom we have studied in the Word of God. Men of renowned; Prophets whose life committed and devoted to God we want to emulate.

Job sat grieving in sack cloth and ashes cutting himself with pieces of pottery, after the Lord, in Job chapters 1 and 2, allowed Satan to first take all his possessions including his children, and then striking his body with painful boils from head to toe.

We readily zero in on the fact that—*"in all this Job did not sin nor charge God with wrong",* according **Job 1:22** and in **Job 2:10b**, *"Shall we indeed accept good from God, and shall we not accept adversity?" In all this Job did not sin with his lips.* This is truly the example of a life entrusted to God. Looking at those passages with a passing glance seems above par on the righteous scale doesn't it?

If we stop at the end of chapter 2 we can in no way identify with the spiritual stature or human nature of this man, but if we journey into chapter 3 suddenly we see a Job that has real earthly responses we can better understand.

Right at the entrance of **Job chapter 3** we witness this disturbing, gut wrenching statement, *"May the day perish on which I was born, and the night in which it was said, 'A male child is conceived.'—"<u>Why did I not die at birth</u>? Why did I not perish when I came from the womb?"* **Job 3:3,11**"

Jobs reactions were very understandable, in the natural. None of us could point the finger of judgment at this man of God. Our reaction, if we are honest, would be much the same. I can attest if it were me, the reaction would be much worse.

Let's look at another icon of the faith. The Prophet Elijah took on the prophets of Baal in a show down on Mount Carmel in a battle of the true power of Almighty God. The end result was the destruction of the four hundred prophets of Baal. When the evil Queen Jezebel heard the news through King Ahab she sent word to Elijah that she was going to take his life. After receiving this letter of threat Elijah fled to Beersheba.

In **1 Kings 19** we find Elijah crumpled on the ground tired, weary, and in despair.   **1 Kings 19:4** records, *"But he himself went a day's journey into the wilderness, and came and sat down under a broom tree. And he prayed that he might die, and said, '<u>It is enough! Now, Lord, take my life</u>, for I am no better than my* *fathers!'"* Again, this is an understandable response. We might question why after witnessing his spiritual boldness when taking on the godless prophets of Baal, but when faced with the possibility of his own demise he recoiled—this we can relate too.

The truth no matter where we are in our spiritual growth Jesus understands our gripe, our complaint, and even our anger. The Lord's shoulders are so large He can handle our emotional outburst. It is OK to question why! It is OK to show our weakness.

Paul wrote these words which included Christ' words to him after the apostle prayed three times for what he called "a thorn in the flesh" to be removed—

2 Corinthians 12:9-10 (NKJV)

⁹ "And He said to me, "My grace is sufficient for you, for My strength is made perfect in weakness." Therefore most gladly I will rather boast in my infirmities, that the power of Christ may rest upon me. ¹⁰ Therefore I take pleasure in infirmities, in reproaches, in needs, in persecutions, in distresses, for Christ's sake. <u>For when I am weak, then I am strong</u>."

Christ hand is not lifted from you because you are angry at your plight and question His reasons. His love for you is immeasurable.

Another truth is that we may never know the reason why! And that is also OK. The lack of a satisfactory answer as far as our finite mind desires does not remove the Lord's sovereignty. But, perhaps if we stop and rest under the tree or in the midst of our own ashes of grief we just might hear Him speak and feel His hand lift us up out of our despair and shroud us with a cloud of peace during our storm.

Going back to the story of Elijah—He thought he was alone; all had been killed that trusted the Lord, but then God spoke—*"Yet I have reserved __seven thousand__ in Israel, all whose knees have not bowed to Baal, and every mouth that has not kissed him."* Elijah was not alone in this fight.

For Job the education came in chapters 38 thru 41. The overall theme?—God's sovereignty. The Lord was there at the beginning of all creation and was with Job now. Job listened and was enlightened. His response was one of humility and comfort in the hands of an All Powerful God, "Then Job answered the Lord and said: *"I know that You can do everything, and that no purpose of Yours can be withheld from You. You asked, 'Who is this who hides counsel without knowledge?' Therefore I have uttered what I did not understand, Things too wonderful for me, which I did not know. Listen, please, and let me speak; You said, 'I will question you, and you shall answer Me.' "I have heard of You by the hearing of the ear,*
but now __my eye sees You__. Therefore I abhor myself, And repent in dust and ashes."

It is OK to feel and express, but as you do, stop, look, and listen. You just might see the Lord's hand in all of it; holding you up and helping you STAND TALL!

Questions to ponder:

1. **What pain am I focusing on today that keeps me from hearing the Lord?**

2. **Whose voice am I listening too, God the Father or the father of lies-(the devil)?**

Additional Scriptural food: 2 Corinthians 4; Hebrews 4:13-15

Day 16: The fight

"Throw the towel", the assistant yells toward the trainer. Trying desperately to raise his voice above the deafening roar of the crowd he shouts again, "Throw in the towel now!" Still the trainer doesn't respond. In a last ditch effort to force his attention the assistant grabs the arm of the man. As the trainer catches his eye, the assistant speaks in a deliberate manner, "What are you waiting for? Our fighter is getting beat senseless out there. Throw in the towel and stop this fight."

With a determination in his voice and an unmovable confidence the trainer spoke, "I know this man—he's not finished— he's got more fight in him!" With a gleam in his eye the trainer continues, "The battles not over! You just watch and see!"

How many times has this scenario played out in your head? How many times have you sat in your own corner of the ring and said, "I'm done! Throw in the towel I can't fight anymore"?

Some time ago in my office as I sat in a puddle of my own self-pity I asked the Lord, "How long do I have to do this?" Jab after jab of doubt, confusion, and uncertainty pounded my head stopping any sense of clarity. I had taken so many blows it seemed that I couldn't lift my hands to fight.

Throughout the day in my head I heard the words, "Give up—throw in the towel—end this fight and move on to something else." Even though I know better I tend to fight with my own brawn. But, then I am reminded of the words of Paul in *2 Corinthians 10:4-6, "For the weapons of our warfare are not carnal but mighty in God for pulling down strongholds, ⁵ casting down arguments and <u>every high thing</u> that exalts itself against the knowledge of God, bringing every thought into captivity to the obedience of Christ, ⁶ and being ready to punish all disobedience when your obedience is fulfilled."*

It's those high things that seem to fly in at us from every angle; thoughts we have placed in the center of our mental room. Like an accent wall all focus is directed to this one thought—like a shrine. We all have those moments when we cannot see past ourselves to the greater good, the greater purpose.

When I took a rest from the mental sparing, the Lord began to speak to me about the high places I had erected in my life as the focal point. Christ reminded me that when the kings of old would want to turn their country around spiritually they would first go after the high places.

In these high places were monuments and altars to false gods. These focal points, in reality, distracted the people from the one true God. They became places of worship.

When Josiah became king he desired to restore true worship to the one true God and restore the covenant. Josiah went after the distracting things—destroyed them.

2 Kings 23:15 says, *"Even the altar at Bethel, the high place made by Jeroboam son of Nebat, who had caused Israel to sin—even that altar and high place he demolished. He burned the high place and ground it to powder, and burned the Asherah pole* (sacred tree or pole that stood near <u>Canaanite</u> religious locations to honor the <u>Ugaritic</u> mother-goddess <u>Asherah</u>, consort of <u>El</u>.) *also."*

In order to restore true worship and clarity of the covenant of God Josiah had to completely destroy those things that had been set up to replace what God had intended for his people.

So often, albeit unintentional, we erect our own Asherah poles that become our focal point and distract us from what God truly desires for us to accomplish for His glory.

We get so overwhelmed by the blows that our enemy is throwing in order to cause us to throw in the towel and run to that monument of distraction we have raised—we eventually run back to what seemed such an easy existence for us.

The Asherah pole may have been attractive in appearance and truthfully didn't require much sacrifice, but it didn't do much either—it simply stood there. The fight we are in, however, requires diligence, perseverance, and faith, but in the end—a crown!

2 Timothy 4:8 says, *"Finally, there is laid up for me the crown of righteousness, which the Lord, the righteous Judge, will give to me on that Day, and not to me only but also to all who have loved His appearing."*

Let us keep up the fight focusing on the win, because as the Word says in—

Revelations 3:12, *"Him who overcomes I will make a pillar in the temple of My God. Never again will he leave it. I will write on him the name of my God and the name of the city of My God, the new Jerusalem, which is coming down out of heaven from my God; and I will also write on Him My new name."* What a promise!

Questions to ponder:

1. **What high places of distraction do I need to tear down in my life?**

2. **What must I do to prepare and win the fight?**

Additional Scriptural food: 1 Samuel 17:47; 2 Timothy 4:1-8

Day 17: To forgive, or not to forgive?—that is the question

Will you forgive me?—Four simple words. Easy for some to utter, for others not so much, but wherever you fall in those two groups those words have at some time fell from your lips. If you are anything like me the memory of that moment is not too distant. But not only have you and I been the producer of this question there is not a one of us that has not been on the receiving end as well.

Lately I have been pondering the depth of this question. There are obviously two answers to these words spoken in every dialect; needed in every culture—Yes or No! When "No" is decided its meaning is clear and understood. The answer "Yes" should follow the same rule. But, does it?

We would hope that when "Yes I forgive you" is uttered it is delivered with confidence, shrouded in truth, and lands with compassion. Unfortunately too often "Yes" is surrendered because we know that is what is expected, especially from a Christian, but deep inside is a cesspool of resentment swirling around in a cauldron of bitterness.

Whether it is a "No", or a falsified "Yes", why is it so difficult for some Christians to fully forgive when forgiveness is the very foundation of our belief. Remember what Jesus spoke as He taught us how to pray in Matthew 6:14-15, *"For if you forgive men their trespasses, your heavenly Father will also forgive you. But if you do not forgive men their trespasses, neither will your Father forgive your trespasses."*

As I sit here and write, an answer to the question "Why" comes to my mind. I believe we struggle with our ability to truly forgive because we forget how far Christ had to reach to pull us out of our sin and imperfection to forgive us.

Continual self-examination reminds us of our human frailty and how we need Christ to forgive us time and time again—and how overjoyed we are to know that He does. Paul's word to the church in Ephesus puts it right in our face in Ephesians 4:32 "And be kind to one another, tenderhearted, forgiving one another, even as God in Christ forgave you."

We reason as if this forgiveness thing is a choice by lumping it with "forgive and forget!" We declare how impossible it is to forget such a wrong done to us. We were never asked to forget. We can't on our own ability—much of what was done to us was probably pretty painful and the hurt runs deep.

The truth is forgiveness is a purposeful act. It may begin seemingly very mechanical—just words, but as we start with the act of confessing, it soon it becomes a part of us. It starts in the mind and ends in the heart.

As we begin by choosing to forgive in time, though you may remember the act, you will notice that the sting has begun to subside.

Since we know that Christ Himself commands us to forgive then how can we not. I know that I Eco what you are thinking right now—I do not want to stand before my Lord Jesus Christ and give an account of an unforgiving heart.

Make the choice today to walk in forgiveness and breath this simple prayer, "Oh Lord help me to forgive as you have forgiven me!

Questions to ponder:

1. Who do I need to forgive?

2. Have I set out to show I forgive?

Additional Scriptural food: Matthew 6:9-15; Matthew 18:21-35

Day 18: Making Amends

Amends: *Something done or given as compensation for a wrong.*

What a daunting task it can be to make an amends to someone we have had a conflict with. Depending on the severity of the abrasion in the relationship it can fill like a batter stepping up to the plate for the fourth time with three strike outs behind him. The since of failure is insurmountable.

"What if they do not except my amends?" you wonder! "Or what if they respond in a less then empathetic way?" These questions are valid and understandable, but ask yourself this question—"What if I do nothing; What if I respond to this fear and intimidation swirling about my head by running and hiding from the responsibility of acting on it? Perhaps it will go away?"

The truth is it never really goes away! Oh, we stuff it down until it becomes out of sight out of mind. This individual has within themselves a box. In that box they tightly pack all of their emotional baggage; hurts and sinful secrets, until one day it resurfaces at the wrong time; then "Blam!"—the lock pops off, and like a volcano it spews guilt, resentment, and bitterness all over everything! When the dust settles and the damage has been done they sweep up the residue, stuff it back in the box, and put a fresh padlock back on it until the next time.

We need to understand that this amends thing isn't just about the other person. It's about you responding in a way that pleases the Lord and breaking spiritual strongholds in your life. Not hiding from it hoping it will fix itself.

The Apostle Paul wrote in **Romans 12:18**, *"If it is possible, as far as it depends on you, live at peace with everyone."* The key phrase in that passage is *"as far as it depends on you."* There is a purposeful effort to be made in order to carry this verse out. It is not coming to you with an expectation of a positive response. It is simply looking at our response.

What are the strong holds that wrap tentacles around our waist holding us back and ultimately are released when we respond as the amender?

1. Guilt

The weight of guilt is like a wetsuit made of steel.

Look what the writer of Hebrews wrote in—

Hebrews 12:1-3 (NKJV)

"Therefore we also, since we are surrounded by so great a cloud of witnesses, let us lay aside every weight, and the sin which so easily ensnares us, and let us run with endurance the race that is set before us,[2] looking unto Jesus, the author and finisher of our faith,

who for the joy that was set before Him endured the cross, despising the shame, and has sat down at the right hand of the throne of God."

It's about laying aside the things that hinder our progression in Christ—in our purpose as believers; keeping our focus on what Christ wants, and when we allow the guilt from the past to hold us back by not seeking to make amends with those who have a hand in the guilt we feel our spiritual growth is stunted.

2. Bitterness

Though you may have been the instigator of the conflict, the role play of their response has left pockets full of seeds of bitterness, assuming something that hasn't happened yet. Living with this constant mental and spiritual battle that begins in the mind and then eventually ending in the heart will rob you of all joy.

Job in his pain and suffering found himself in this extreme condition. Look at the statement he makes in **Job 10:1 (NKJV)**

"My soul loathes my life;
I will give free course to my complaint,
I will speak in the bitterness of my soul."

Job did not understand what was going on, so much so he even desired to die. His focus was completely on his state at the moment. I think you and I could understand this bitterness given the circumstances. But, I think it even goes deeper than that for Job. He fear this day would come. There was pre-thought. "What if?" **Job**

3:25 (NKJV) *"For the thing I greatly feared has come upon me, and what I dreaded has happened to me."*

Even as righteous as Job was he had the human tendency as you and I do to get distracted with life's hardships, and when we feel injustice has been done if we are not careful bitterness can feel the hole where loss has occurred.

3. Pride

Pride leads to acceptance and justification of our feelings.

If we are seeking amends with someone involved in our hurt it doesn't matter how the individual responds in the forgiveness process. You have done your part. You have walked out Romans 12:18, *"If it is possible, as far as it depends on you, live at peace with everyone."* and you are responding to the words of Jesus in **Matthew 5:23-25** *"Therefore if you bring your gift to the altar, and there remember that <u>your brother has something against you</u>, leave your gift there before the altar, and go your way. First be reconciled to your brother, and then come and offer your gift. Agree with your adversary quickly, while you are on the way with him, lest your adversary deliver you to the judge, the judge hand you over to the officer, and you be thrown into prison."*

Friend if we desire to live a spiritually prosperous life we need to be willing to stand to our feet and say "Lord, if I have caused an offense and need to make an amends give me the courage to go to my brother, or sister and genuinely make it right. You will be amazed at the release generated from that, in retrospect, simple action of making amends.

Questions to ponder:

1. **What offense am I holding on too?**

2. **Who do I need to seek out in order to make amends?**

   Additional Scriptural food: Proverbs 18:19; Matthew 7:3-5; Romans 14:9-11

Day 19: Who hindered you?

"Things were going so well", he thought. "They were growing in their faith; understanding the basic truth of the freedom of the Gospel of Christ—and then someone threw a wrench in the works causing these new ones to fall backward into the bondage of religious mutilation to mark who they are; to somehow through the law commanded markings they are justified."

These frustrations belonged to the Apostle Paul leading him to write to his beloved Galatians to somehow redirect them back to the justification by faith in Christ, reminding them to simply return to the message he had preached; a gospel of grace and mercy.

We see Paul's urgent tone to these new converts in Galatians 5:7-12 *"You ran well. Who hindered you from obeying the truth? [8] This persuasion does not come from Him who calls you. [9] A little leaven leavens the whole lump. [10] I have confidence in you, in the Lord, that you will have no other mind; but he who troubles you shall bear his judgment, whoever he is. [11] And I, brethren, if I still preach circumcision, why do I still suffer persecution? Then the offense of the cross has ceased. [12] I could wish that those who trouble you would even cut themselves off!"*

These Galatians had stepped back into a religiosity of sorts. Let's bring the idea into a more modern understanding—"if I look the part and engage in all the Christian-eze then I am". This theology far removes the truthful teachings of Paul to Titus in Titus

3:4-6 *"But when the kindness and the love of God our Savior toward man appeared, ⁵ not by works of righteousness which we have done, but according to His mercy He saved us, through the washing of regeneration and renewing of the Holy Spirit, ⁶ whom He poured out on us abundantly through Jesus Christ our Savior,"*

As you and I delve into Scripture we come to the understanding that there is nothing you and I can do to qualify to receive this precious gift of mercy and regeneration. It was provided for us on the cross at Calvary over two thousand years ago. We didn't deserve it. Christ willingly provided it to an undeserving mankind. That is what makes it so amazing.

Then, there is the other extreme to the truth of mercy; those who use the term religiosity as a cop out. These individuals do not want requirements or accountability. They want freedom without boundaries. Paul addresses this very point farther down in his letter to the **Galatians** in Chapter 5 verse 13, *"For you, brethren, have been called to liberty; only do not use liberty as an opportunity for the flesh, but through love serve one another."*

There are requirements for the believer—and thankfully boundaries. Can you imagine a people without boundaries or requirements?—If you can, then you can envision total chaos and a lack of restraint. Micah 6:8 says, *"He has shown you, O man, what is good; and what does the Lord require of you but to do justly, to love mercy, and to walk humbly with your God?"* And Peter reminds us in his first letter, **1 Peter 1:13-16 *"Therefore gird up the*** *loins of your mind, be sober, and rest your hope fully upon the grace that is to be brought to you at the revelation of Jesus Christ; ¹⁴ as obedient children, not conforming yourselves to the former lusts, as in your ignorance; ¹⁵ but as He who called you is holy, you also be holy in all your conduct,¹⁶ because it is written, "Be holy, for I am holy."*

Yes we live within the grace and mercy of the Lord, but let's always remember that we are to—*"Pursue peace with all people, and holiness, without which no one will see the Lord:"* **Hebrews 12:14**

Questions to ponder:

1. **Am I passionate in my relationship with Christ or merely religious?**

2. **What must I lay down in order to surrender to get back on track with the Lord?**

   Additional Scriptural food: Psalm 73:26; Matthew 16:24; Romans 3:1-26

Day 20: Determined to draw near (The pursuit of Christ)

I sat alone in an open room taking my usual spot at one of three circular tables pushed together to form an octagon shape. I waited for the nine gentlemen that would fill the remaining chairs in the circle.

Coming to the meeting unsure what the Lord would have me teach, there was a since of grieving inside. I could not really pin point what was going on. Oh I had an idea of part of its origin, but it was deeper than my surface emotions. Not knowing the direction the Lord was going to lead I opened my Bible and began to thumb through its pages until my eyes were drawn to a particular passage.

The Scripture I was glued to was **Hebrews 10:19-23,** *"Therefore, brethren, having boldness to enter the Holiest by the blood of Jesus, [20] by a new and living way which He consecrated for us, through the veil, that is, His flesh, [21] and having a High Priest over the house of God, [22] let us draw near with a true heart in full assurance of faith, having our hearts sprinkled from an evil conscience and our bodies washed with pure water. [23] Let us hold fast the confession of our hope without wavering, for He who promised is faithful."*

In that entire paragraph four words seemed to jump off the page. These words are found in the beginning of **Verse 22,** *"Let us* *draw near…"* I knew at that instance the Lord was giving me the foundation of discussion He had chosen for the men that night. Then a question followed; a question that I would ask the men, but not before asking myself. In my head came these words, "What does drawing near look like?"

When we look at this seemingly simple statement we come to conclusions that are largely based on familiar traditions and routines. One may envision the corporate worship service and altar gathering as an example of drawing near. But is that all it takes?

As those questions spun around my head and then out of my mouth to the listening ears of the men that gathered that evening the Lord brought me to a dramatic scene in His Word. This story opened our eyes to the sacrificial pursuit of Jesus God desires from His children.

The event is found in **Luke 8:43-48** *"Now a woman, having a flow of blood for twelve years, who had spent all her livelihood on physicians and could not be healed by any, [44] came from behind and touched the border of His garment. And immediately her flow of blood stopped. [45] And Jesus said, "Who touched Me?"*

When all denied it, Peter and those with him said, "Master, the multitudes throng and press You, and You say, 'Who touched Me?'" [46] But Jesus said, "Somebody touched Me, for I perceived power going out from Me." [47] Now when the woman saw that she was not hidden, she came trembling; and falling down before Him, she declared to Him in the presence of all the people the reason she had touched Him and how she was healed immediately. [48] *And He said to her, "Daughter, be of good cheer; your faith has made you well. Go in peace."*

Think about that story for a moment. What did it take for her to get to Jesus? The story paints the picture of the position she must have been in to grab the boarders or hem of Christ' robe. I see her as nearly prostrate; pushing her way through, nearly at a crawl.

Can you imagine the effort she had to put forth to get to the feet of Jesus? She must have been bumped and kicked as she nudged her way along the feet of the multitude. Beyond those few moments of discomfort there was her physical condition. This poor woman had been bleeding for twelve years. She was probably suffering from a condition known as anemia which would certainly result in extreme lethargy.

In the midst of all of these obstacles this woman was determined. Nothing was going to stop her from getting to the one who could heal and bless her. She didn't let what seemed impossible to keep her back; not the people, her status in society, nor her physical condition. She needed to get close to the source and was determined no matter the cost.

It is not uncommon to hear fellow believers declare that they long to draw nearer to the Lord. In fact I would venture to say there is not a Christian alive that has not echoed that sentiment. But, when it comes to the effort that is required we fall short and remain in our cocoon of comfort. "Give me my cozy feelings and splash the blessings upon me, but don't make me work for it. I don't want to be kicked by the crowd—I don't want people to stare at me while I break and linger at the altar as if I'm desperate."

The woman we just read about was so desperate to get near Jesus she didn't care what people thought. "I need my moment with the master" was all the woman must have been thinking.

As you are reading this you may be going through your own desperate situation. You are unclear what to do. Push through the crowd with determination my friend forgetting who is around you. The hem of the creator is in reach.

James reminded us in **James 4:8** how it works. He said, *"Draw near to God and He will draw near to you. Cleanse your hands, you sinners; and purify your hearts, you double-minded."* As we move toward Christ we can be assured He is going to move toward us, filling us with His presence. But look at the preparation James describes as we move toward the Lord, *"Cleanse your hands, you sinners; and purify your hearts, you double-minded."*

We need to come before the Lord empty, broken, and spilled out; releasing everything at the feet of Jesus. And as we do we can hear Jesus say, *"...be of good cheer; your faith has made you well. Go in peace."*

Questions to ponder:

1. What must I do to draw nearer to Christ?

2. What does clean hands and a pure heart look like for me?

   Additional Scriptural food: Psalm 51:16-17; 1Timothy 6:11; 2 Timothy 2:22; Hebrews 12:12-17

Day 21: A giant in every town

How big does something really have to be to be considered a giant? I think the answer to that question is simply this—anything that appears bigger than I am; any person, place, or thing. Truthfully there are many things in each of our lives that we would consider giants—a health condition, financial obstacle, and even relationships. But I think the biggest giant of all can be when the Lord calls us to do something that seems so beyond whom we are.

A couple weeks ago I was reading in Deuteronomy where Moses recounted the rebellion of the children of Israel. How they refused to go into the Promised Land because of a bad report brought back to them by ten of the twelve men sent to spy out the land. It reads in **Deuteronomy 1:28**, *"Where can we go up? Our brethren have discouraged our hearts, saying, "The people are greater and taller than we; the cities are great and fortified up to heaven; moreover we have seen the sons of the Anakim there."'* That statement was all the people could focus on. The Israelites ears were not tuned into the aforementioned bounty of the land, *"'it is* **a good land which the LORD our God is giving us.',** but rather their eyes were fixed on the stature of the men in the town they were called to possess.

As a man I'm not quick to judge that response. In fact I can relate to it, and perhaps you can too. We will be surrounded by many good things, but it is that one big looming problem that upsets the whole cart. I can easily be distracted by this one in your face seemingly unmovable obstacle. I get these Israelites. They know what God is saying, but they can't get passed what they are seeing. The command comes flooding in and so does the doubt and discouragement; *"Why is God doing this?" "There is just no way we will overcome what we know to be standing in our way!"*

Yet, there were two out of all the people, Caleb and Joshua, who believed differently. What did they see that the others didn't? Oh, they saw the giants—they knew they were there. But there focus was on the promise made by Jehovah. These men believed in its fulfillment. Why? Because the Lord spoke it, and their vision of the pursuit was through God's infinite eyes not their finite ones. Because of the Israelites lack of faith in the fulfillment of God's promise that generation never saw the prosperity God intended, only Caleb, Joshua, and the coming up generation.

As we continue to read in **Deuteronomy chapters 2 to 3** we read how the Israelites traveled around in circles as the next generation grew. In their journey they passed other towns which had giants as well. We read this statement—*"a people as great and numerous and tall as the Anakim. They were also regarded as giants, like the Anakim, but the Moabites call them Emim".* (**Deuteronomy 2:10, 11**) Then they came near the people of Ammon, and again there were giants. This time they were given the name *"Zamzummim"*(**Deuteronomy 2:20**)

So often we will continue focusing on the giants in our life—they look the same, but we give them different names. They are simply distractions; tools of Satan to discourage us and to take our eyes off of the promise of God. We forget who we are in Christ. We are blinded to the power we have over these obstacles through Jesus name.

As we look at these stories in God's Word it all has to do with perspective. Do we look through our fleshly eyes or through the eyes of the one who spoke the world into existence? It reminds me of the futuristic prophetic words of Isaiah describing our response when we as believers will see Satan visibly for the first time—*"Those who see you will gaze at you,*
And consider you, saying: 'Is this the man who made the earth tremble, who shook kingdoms.." **Isaiah 14:6**. Friends it is all about perspective. How do we see what is ahead of us or where we are going?

If we are paying attention own eyes will deceive us. I need to see through the eyes of Jesus! Pray for spiritual blinders so that you are not tempted to look to the right or the left, but rather straight ahead to the victory and take the land the Lord has established for you.

Questions to ponder:

1. What are the giants in my life that distract me from taking the land the Lord has set before me?

2. What or to whom do I place my trust?

Additional Scriptural food: Psalm 4:4-6; Psalm 13; Ephesians 6:10-20

Day 22: Prostrate Prayer (Positioned for victory)

I lay in bed one night trying desperately to fall asleep. I wanted the day to end and hoping for a more productive day when the sun rose the following morning—it would be Sunday after all. What was keeping me from slumber? My self—my own thoughts!

I looked over at my wife Kim—she had already made it to the mysterious land of dreams. Why couldn't I? Because I had succumbed to an inner battle many of us fight in the wee hours of the night if we allow it. It's the fight of discouragement, depression, and self-worth.

In that lonely moment in the dark I cried out to the Lord, "Father I am fifty-one years" old—(many of you will laugh at that notion—you've seen that one come and go) I'm no longer fifty I am in my fifties. I continued, "What are you doing?" I felt so unsure of anything—physically, financially, as well as direction in ministry. This wave of discouragement kept beating against me until I finally fell asleep.

As I slept I had a dream. In this dream I was in a church service. The building was familiar in thought but not in appearance. I was asked if I would preach the last part of the message which would include the altar call. This request was not strange in itself since I had in reality been asked to do that very thing before.

What was unusual was what I didn't have. I approached the pulpit with no notes and no Bible. All that I had with me was an empty file folder (I have come to understand that the empty folder represented the fact that I had no agenda.

I looked up toward the ceiling and breathed a prayer, "Father, what do you want me to say to these people?" Suddenly the anointing fell and I began to speak fluently on the goodness of God. Remember I went to bed in despair and now I am preaching on the Lord's goodness and His faithfulness.

As soon as the message concluded I woke up. I went about my usual Sunday morning routine as my wife was going about hers. Sitting at my desk reading my e-mail while eating breakfast the Lord began to speak clearly to my heart—

"Here is how you break the strongholds of discouragement, depression, and fear. I want you to return to a prostrate prayer life as opposed to a distractive prayer life."

The Lord began to show me what a distractive prayer life was. It is a prayer life that is filled with chaos. Prayers of desperation—consumed with panic. It is a communication that is me focused.

To prostrate our self before the Lord is to simply humbly surrender all that I am to him. It becomes all about pleasing Jesus. In Deuteronomy 9 the Israelites were in rebellion again so Moses responded in hopes that God would turn from his wrath:

Deuteronomy 9:24-26 records Moses words—

"You have been rebellious against the Lord from the day that I knew you. ²⁵ "Thus I <u>prostrated</u> myself before the Lord; forty days and forty nights <u>I kept prostrating</u> myself, because the Lord had said He would destroy you. ²⁶ Therefore I prayed to the Lord, and said: 'O Lord God, do not destroy Your people and Your inheritance whom You have redeemed through Your greatness, whom You have brought out of Egypt with a mighty hand."

Moses kept prostrating himself until He heard from God. He lowered himself into the presence of the Lord, and God was pleased and stayed his hand again. King David gave a similar response was when faced with the consequences of his sin with Bathsheba. The Lord was going to take the child's life that was born to David and Bathsheba. Look at the account in—

2 Samuel 12:15b-23

"And the Lord struck the child that Uriah's wife bore to David, and it became ill. ¹⁶ David therefore pleaded with God for the child, and David fasted and went in and lay all night on the ground. ¹⁷ So the elders of his house arose and went to him, to raise him up from the ground. But he would not, nor did he eat food with them. ¹⁸ Then on the seventh day it came to pass that the child died. And the servants of David were afraid to tell him that the child was dead. For they said, "Indeed, while the child was alive, we spoke to him, and he would not heed our voice. How can we tell him

that the child is dead? He may do some harm!"

[19] When David saw that his servants were whispering, David perceived that the child was dead. Therefore David said to his servants, "Is the child dead?"

And they said, "He is dead."

[20] So David arose from the ground, washed and anointed himself, and changed his clothes; and he went into the house of the Lord and worshiped. Then he went to his own house; and when he requested, they set food before him, and he ate. [21] Then his servants said to him, "What is this that you have done? You fasted and wept for the child while he was alive, but when the child died, you arose and ate food." [22] And he said, "While the child was alive, I fasted and wept; for I said, 'Who can tell whether the Lord will be gracious to me, that the child may live?' [23] But now he is dead; why should I fast? Can I bring him back again? I shall go to him, but he shall not return to me."

The answer from spending time in God's presence in humility wasn't the response David hoped for, but when it was given he accepted it.

I have to admit I still am trying to fully understand what a prostrate prayer life looks like, but the Lord has brought to my understanding that it isn't about me and that it is not about the position of my body, but the position of my heart. I ask you today friend—will you journey with me to discover and acquire a prostrate prayer life?

Question to ponder:

What is the prayerful condition of my heart; distractive or prostrate?

Additional Scriptural food: Matthew 6:5-15; Acts 12:4-6

Day 23: Walk in the Spirit

As I sat early one morning in the back stock room of the store I managed at the time preparing to open the doors for the day's business I raised my hands and began to ask for the Lord's favor. Getting up and walking around the store I began to pray in the Spirit. Suddenly, I felt a lift inside replacing the weariness I felt on my drive to the mall, when **Galatians 5:16-18** came to my mind,

[16] "I say then: Walk in the Spirit, and you shall not fulfill the lust of the flesh. [17] for the flesh lusts against the Spirit, and the Spirit against the flesh; and these are contrary to one another, so that you do not do the things that you wish. [18] But if you are led by the Spirit, you are not under the law."

Something clicked in me. So often we as Christians splash around in the wading pool of Scripture never allowing its current to catch us in the rip tide—pulling us down to the depth of understanding.

Even as I pen these words I have to restrain the tears (I am at work after all) of gratitude that desire to burst forth from my eyes. My attention had been detoured to a new place—a place it should always remain. But, the road I most travel, as many of you who are reading this may relate, is one of self-absorption.

When we see the statement Paul made, *"fulfilling the lusts of the flesh"* what often comes to some is that it refers to an immoral act or thought—when in essence it is *anything* that gratifies me—how I desire to respond to any given situation.

Today, for me, it is about a new consumption—a consumption of walking under the canopy of the Holy Ghost and walking out from underneath the cloud of self-indulgence.

As a reactor to any given situation I often believe that I need to prove my right and defend *my honor*, instead of simply walking in the glory of the Spirit—knowing that if I follow where He leads I am always going in the right direction.

Paul said it so powerfully at the end of this passage, *"you are not under the law."* What does that mean? I believe it is saying that our walking no longer is weighted by religious actions, but rather spiritual vitality—putting a spring in your step and a song in your heart.

The truth is, that situation you are going through, may still be there and as real as ever, but it no longer deters you for we know—

"God is our refuge and strength,
A very present help in trouble.
² Therefore we will not fear,
Even though the earth be removed,
And though the mountains be carried into the midst of the sea;

³ Though its waters roar and be troubled,
Though the mountains shake with its swelling. Selah

Psalm 46:1-3

Change your consumption friend. Take your eyes off of your situation to the movement of The Spirit--following where He leads-- *"Now the Lord is the Spirit; and where the Spirit of the Lord is, there is liberty."* **2 Corinthians 3:17**

I know how consuming life's circumstances can be. Knowing this, we have to purposefully choose to take those monumental moments and reenergize before the Lord; to be empowered to "walk in The Spirit" Then, watch where the Spirit leads, and you will be like a child on a dirt trail stepping in his father's foot prints.

Questions to ponder:

1. How have I been side track in my walk with the Lord?

2. Have I reenergized my spirit at the Lord's feet today?

Additional Scriptural food: Acts 6:8-15; Acts 8:26-40; Acts 16:6-8

Day 24: The Pursuit of Fullness

Fullness is a common desire of every human being, and most will do what ever it takes to acquire it. Whether it is a full bank account, full belly, or a full gas tank. We grapple in our pursuit of our wants and necessities; succeeding in our grasp for some and falling short in our reach for others, but there is a fullness within reach of our heart--yet so few of us put forth the effort required to obtain it. Look at the Apostle Paul's letter to the Ephesians—

Ephesians 3:8-19

"To me, who am less than the least of all the saints, this grace was given, that I should preach among the Gentiles the unsearchable riches of Christ, and to make all see what is the fellowship of the mystery, which from the beginning of the ages has been hidden in God who created all things through Jesus Chris; to the intent that now the manifold wisdom of God might be made known by the church to the principalities and powers in the heavenly places, according to the eternal purpose which He accomplished in Christ Jesus our Lord, in whom we have boldness and access with confidence through faith in Him. 13 Therefore I ask that you do not lose heart at my tribulations for you, which is your glory.

"For this reason I bow my knees to the Father of our Lord Jesus Christ, from whom the whole family in heaven and earth is named,

that He would grant you, according to the riches of His glory, to be strengthened with might through His Spirit in the inner man, that Christ may dwell in your hearts through faith; that you, being rooted and grounded in love, may be able to comprehend with all the saints what is the width and length and depth and height—to know the love of Christ which passes knowledge; that you may be filled with all the <u>fullness of God</u>."

Having fullness is being filled to Capacity. I probably echo what you are thinking right now—"I want to be filled to capacity with the glory of God". The song that continues to ring in my ear as I write is the old familiar tune those of us who are fifty some things remember frequently sung in church—

"Fill my cup Lord, I lift it up Lord. Come and quench this thirsting of my soul
Bread of heaven feed me till I want no more. Here's my cup, fill it up and make me whole."

It is a great tune for sure, but so often we are so content with siting there in our church pew holding our cup in the air hoping for a drop or two. The idea of making an effort to pursue after the source is outside of our traditional, or dare I say, religious rhetoric we are accustom too.

Let's look at the word pursuit for a moment. It is one of those action words. It simply means **"The act of chasing after something!"**
To acquire the fullness of God requires a deliberate act of

pursuing.   In the pursuit of The Fullness of God there are three actions we as believers must engage in.   Let's look at them—

1. The Action of Removal

During my devotions one morning I turned to the book Ezekiel.   I began to read chapter 14.   As I scanned the verses the Lord began to speak to me and open my eyes to something I had not paid attention to before.   Look what the prophet Ezekiel writes—
Ezekiel 14:1-5,

"Now some of the elders of Israel came to me and sat before me. 2 And the word of the Lord came to me, saying, 3 "Son of man, these men have set up their idols in their hearts, and put before them that which causes them to stumble into iniquity. Should I let Myself be inquired of at all by them?
4 "Therefore speak to them, and say to them, 'Thus says the Lord God: "Everyone of the house of Israel who sets up his idols in his heart, and puts before him what causes him to stumble into iniquity, and then comes to the prophet, I the Lord will answer him who comes, according to the multitude of his idols, 5 that I may seize the house of Israel by their heart, because they are all estranged from Me by their idols."'

You like me have probably asked yourself, "What is it that keeps me from walking in the fullness of the Lord? Why can I not hear Him clearly?"

Have you ever thought that it may be caused by the idols you have placed before the Lord in your life? I hadn't that about it to

the extent I am now since the Lord opened this scripture to me.
Sobering, isn't it?

All these thoughts and practices that are distractions in our life keeping us from a sharper focus on the Lord occupy us in such a way that we stumble into spiritual dysfunction.

What we need is a spiritual wreaking ball to tear down the old dilapidated fortress to make room for what the Lord really wants to place in that spot.

Some of these distraction are obvious, but passed off as just a part of life so we don't classify them as idols.

Here is just a few:

A. Financial--the fear of a lack.

B. Physical--the fear of not being able.

C. Relationship--the fear of being alone, or not being regarded.

D. Or how about fear itself--the fear of being afraid.

Don't get me wrong I don't invalidate anyone of these--they are real and painful, but if allowed they can become the center of our world and Jesus wants to be that.

There is another action that immediately follows the removal—

2. The Action of choice

Look at what Joshua wrote in—

Joshua 24:14,15

"Now therefore, fear the Lord, serve Him in sincerity and in truth, and put away the gods which your fathers served on the other side

of the River and in Egypt. Serve the Lord! And if it seems evil to you to serve the Lord, <u>choose for yourselves</u> this day whom you will serve, whether the gods which your fathers served that were on the other side of the River, or the gods of the Amorites, in whose land you dwell. But as for me and my house, we will serve the Lord."

It's all about the chose. Today you chose to get out of bed; you chose to take a shower before work (let's hope you made that chose); you choose to get in the car on Sunday morning and get your family to church, and you choose to worship.

On the other end of the spectrum you choose to be apathetic, and you choose to focus on yourself. It takes an effort to retrain our thinking from the daily habits we have allowed into our life. We need to become God centered not self-centered. It's all about changing our obsession--which brings us to our final action--

The Act of Determination
Determination is: A Firmness of Purpose
 Look at **what Isaiah 50:7** says,*"For the Lord God will help Me; therefore I will not be disgraced; therefore I have set My face like a flint, and I know that I will not be ashamed."*

Friend we need to set our gaze, our focus on what we are trying to accomplish in Christ; who we are in the Lord. If you are simply satisfied with the status-quo then that is where you will remain, but if you desire the fullness of the Lord you must run after it with purpose.

When Isaiah talked about setting his *"face like a flint"* he was saying that he had become hardened against all opposition; resolute and undaunted; constant and unmoved by the words and blows of men; not to be browbeaten, or put out of countenance, by anything they can say or do.

How amazing it would be if we as the church of Jesus Christ could be fanatically determined in pursuing the Fullness of the Lord! Think about it!

Question to ponder:

1. **What have I set up as an idol in my life that hinders my pursuit of the Fullness of the Lord?**

2. **What must I choose today to walk in the fullness of the Lord?**

Additional Scriptural food: Psalm 17:2-4; Daniel 1:7-9

Day 25: From Darkness to Kingdom

Do you ever just sit and contemplate in amazement about where The Lord has brought you from? The dark gloominess of sin—a hopeless place of despair and utter failure are descriptions, while negative for us to read in print, do not illustrate accurately enough the murky pool we floundered in.

We all began in the above swampy state where Christ reached down and lifted us out. Some of us walked the glory road only to return to that state of wickedness like "*A dog returns to its vomit…*" 2 Peter 2:22a. Yet, amidst all the ugliness and chaos of sin Jesus' hand still found us and brought us back time and time again— from sins so great most of us would turn our back on that soul and say, "that's just too bad."

Some time ago as I sat at the table eating breakfast while reading my devotions I was faced with the reality of God's amazing ability to transcend all human understanding and take what "the devil meant for harm and to turn it around for God's good."

We all are very familiar with the story of David and his sin with Bathsheba and multiplying it with the murder of Bathsheba's husband Uriah in 2 Samuel 11. **Psalm 51:1-19** is the prayer of repentance penned in response to the prophet Nathan coming into the King and exposing his sin.

"Have mercy upon me, O God, according to Your loving kindness; according to the multitude of Your tender mercies, blot out my

transgressions. Wash me thoroughly from my iniquity,
And cleanse me from my sin. For I acknowledge my
transgressions, and my sin is always before me.
Against You, You only, have I sinned, and done this evil in Your
sight--that You may be found just when You speak, and blameless
when You judge.

Behold, I was brought forth in iniquity, and in sin my
mother conceived me. Behold, You desire truth in the inward
parts, and in the hidden part You will make me to know wisdom.

Purge me with hyssop, and I shall be clean; wash me, and I
shall be whiter than snow. Make me hear joy and gladness,
that the bones You have broken may rejoice. hide Your face from
my sins, and blot out all my iniquities.

Create in me a clean heart, O God, and renew a steadfast
spirit within me. Do not cast me away from Your presence, and do
not take Your Holy Spirit from me. Restore to me the joy of Your
salvation, and uphold me by Your generous Spirit. Then I will
teach transgressors Your ways, and sinners shall be converted to
You.

Deliver me from the guilt of bloodshed, O God, the God of
my salvation, and my tongue shall sing aloud of Your
righteousness. O Lord, open my lips,
And my mouth shall show forth Your praise. For You do not
desire sacrifice, or else I would give it; You do not delight in burnt
offering. The sacrifices of God are a broken spirit,
A broken and a contrite heart--these, O God, You will not despise.

Do good in Your good pleasure to Zion; build the walls of Jerusalem. Then You shall be pleased with the sacrifices of righteousness, with burnt offering and whole burnt offering; then they shall offer bulls on Your altar."

I personally have spent much time on the essence of this passage witnessing the genuineness of King David's prayer. I find myself often using psalm as a guide for the repentant heart. But after my time in the word that morning an even greater understanding of God's amazing restorative nature came flooding into my mind which brought to my mind this question—

What did God do that was so utterly mind boggling and amazing?

I began to look at the succession of King David's throne— whom it was that followed his rule. As we read in 2 Samuel we discover that David's quiver was full.

The following names were David's sons:

Amnon, , Daniel, Absalom, Adonijah, Shephatiah, Ithream,

Shimea, Shobab, Nathan, and Solomon—four by Bathsheba—

Also Ibhar, Elishama, Eliphelet, Nogah, Nepheg, Japhia, Elishama, Eliada, and Eliphelet—nine in all. These were all the sons of David, besides the sons of the concubines, and Tamar their sister.

We can clearly see that David had his share of children and we know that it was the 10th child who was chosen to succeed his father—Look at what **1 Kings 1:28-31** says,

"Then King David answered and said, "Call Bathsheba to me." So she came into the king's presence and stood before the king. 29 And the king took an oath and said, "As the Lord lives, who has redeemed my life from every distress, 30 just as I swore to you by the Lord God of Israel, saying, 'Assuredly Solomon your son shall be king after me, and he shall sit on my throne in my place,' so I certainly will do this day."

31 Then Bathsheba bowed with her face to the earth, and paid homage to the king, and said, "Let my lord King David live forever!"

The succession to David's throne didn't follow the natural rule of passing the kingly torch. Tradition would say that the first born Amnon would have been in line to assume the kingship upon his father David's death, but that was not in God's plan.

What was so significant about the choice?

Never before have I been so impacted on who the Lord chose to succeed David. I've always thought of Solomon as a great king because of the Lord's anointing on his life, but there is a greater message here—a true message of restoration.

It is a message of taking something that was headed for destruction and resurrecting it to establish a kingdom.

What do I mean by that?

It's all about where Solomon came from—

Solomon came from Bathsheba not one of David's other wives. He was born from the woman David took by deception and murder, yet following the repentance God began to reestablished what he had begun with David—**A lasting kingdom!**

Romans 11:28-32 says,

"Concerning the gospel they (Jews) are enemies for your sake, but concerning the election they are beloved for the sake of the fathers. 29 <u>For the gifts and the calling of God are irrevocable</u>. 30 For as you were once disobedient to God, yet have now obtained mercy through their disobedience, 31 even so these also have now been disobedient, that through the mercy shown you they also may obtain mercy. 32 For God has committed them all to disobedience, that He might have mercy on all."

The mercy and restoration of the Lord in response to repentance is beyond comprehension. What the Lord began to show me was that he took a dark moment in David's life and recreated a kingdom.

In much the same way He does that with in each of us as we repent and turn our life over to Christ. Thank about that—He takes our shattered life; the life headed for destruction, and creates a kingdom out of it. Jesus spoke these words in
Luke 17:21b, *"For indeed, the kingdom of God is within you."*

The truth is--There is an abundant life after sin should we turn everything over to The Lord. God will take your seemingly hopeless and dark life and create a prosperous kingdom for His glory.

Praise, honor, and glory to Jesus!!

Question to ponder:

What has God turned around in my life that the enemy meant for bad to make it good?

Additional Scriptural food: Psalm 107:1-3; Isaiah 43:1-3; Lamentations 3:57-59; Galatians 3:12-14

Day 26: Even Though

"Help me Lord, please help me!" These six words of desperation are sometimes all we can manage when hard times come—times so out of our control we just don't know what to say. Can you relate to that feeling? I know I can. And in those moments I try to figure out the cause, who or what's to blame and a solution in order to fix the problem—I am a man after all. Isn't it in our DNA to be the rescuer? We are a super hero—at least in our own heads.

The truth is every time we set out to solve a problem on our own we fail, and the problem only becomes magnified. It is like a person who thinks in his head he can rebuild an engine, but he has never picked up a wrench nor does he have a step by step instructional manual. The outcome of such an endeavor would most likely prove disastrous.

The Psalmist wrote in **Psalm 46:1-3 (NKJV)**

"God is our refuge and strength, a very present help in trouble. Therefore we will not fear, even though the earth be removed, and though the mountains be carried into the midst of the sea; though its waters roar and be troubled, though the mountains shake with its swelling. Selah"

A key statement in this passage is ***Even though***. The writer gives us the promise that the Lord will help us, but does not lead us to believe that the trouble will be removed. What does occur is the holding of the hand and leading us through our troubled situation.

Most of us are familiar with this statement written by King David in—

Psalm 23:4,
"Yea (even), though I walk through the valley of the shadow of death,
I will fear no evil; for You are with me; Your rod and Your staff, they comfort me."

This passage illuminates the same understanding that we *may* walk that road of sickness, pain, or even death, but through it all we have the <u>assurance</u> just as David did that God is with us (Emanuel).

Assurance is another element that most of us have a hard time really embracing. Oh, we know what this word means—"A declaration that inspires or is intended to inspire confidence." But to truly live out that level of confidence is something else altogether.

So what is the hang-up?
Paul wrote to the church in Rome these words--
Romans 10:8-10 (NKJV)
8 "But what does it say? "The word is near you, in your mouth and in your heart" (that is, the word of faith which we preach):9 that if

you confess with your mouth the Lord Jesus and believe in your heart that God has raised Him from the dead, you will be saved. 10 For with the heart one believes unto righteousness, and with the mouth confession is made unto salvation."

And again to the church at Corinth he writes—

1 Corinthians 15:57 (NKJV)

"But thanks be to God, who gives us the victory through our Lord Jesus Christ."

If we look in the Greek the word for Lord is *Kurios* which translates *Supreme Authority*. We as believers tend to walk in defeat because we do not grasped the reality that Jesus is The Lord of our life—Supreme Authority!

Jesus declared in **John 16:33--**

John 16:33 (NKJV)

"These things I have spoken to you, that in Me you may have peace. In the world you will have tribulation; but be of good cheer, I have overcome the world."

We need to understand the fact that Christ has overcome our trial. He has us in the palm of His hand and we are never out of His sight. Let me close with this verse written by the prophet Isaiah when he was talking to the people about their separation from God; why they couldn't hear him. It was not God. It was the condition of their heart, but he began his letter with this fact—

Isaiah 59:1 (NKJV)

"Behold, the Lord's hand is not shortened, that it cannot save; nor His ear heavy, that it cannot hear."

We need to understand this fact—that if we remain faithful and yielded to Christ, no matter our situation we will have the ability to walk in the assurance that the Lord is going before us, because our spiritual eyes are opened and not clouded with self-pity.

Knowing this truth we can move ahead with a mind and heart like Christ—that though He faced a greater persecution and sacrifice than you and I will ever face prayed in the Garden, *"...nevertheless not My will, but Yours, be done."* **Luke 22:42b**

May the Lord bless you greatly as you press on in your journey!

Questions to ponder:

1. Have I surrendered today my trials to the Lord?

2. Have I made Jesus The Lord of my life (Supreme Authority)?

Additional Scriptural food: James 1:1-8; James 1:12; 1 Peter 1:3-9

Day 27: Watch and Pray

1 Thessalonians 4:13-18 says,

"But I do not want you to be ignorant, brethren, concerning those who have fallen asleep, lest you sorrow as others who have no hope. [14] For if we believe that Jesus died and rose again, even so God will bring with Him those who sleep in Jesus. [15] For this we say to you by the word of the Lord, that we who are alive and remain until the coming of the Lord will by no means precede those who are asleep. [16] For the Lord Himself will descend from heaven with a shout, with the voice of an archangel, and with the trumpet of God. And the dead in Christ will rise first. [17] Then we who are alive and remain shall be caught up together with them in the clouds to meet the Lord in the air. And thus we shall always be with the Lord. [18] Therefore comfort one another with these words."

The coming of Christ!

What an amazing topic to discuss on any given day. For those of us who have accepted Christ as our Lord and savior this subject sparks anticipation like no other. We are as **Titus 2:13 says,** [13] **"looking for the <u>blessed hope</u> and glorious appearing of our great God and Savior Jesus Christ..."**

However you believe the timing of the coming of the Lord is to occur;

Pre-Tribulation Rapture: (Before the tribulation period)

Mid-Tribulation Rapture: (Three-and-half years into the Tribulation just before the Great Tribulation)

Post-Tribulation Rapture: (Following the Great Tribulation and then immediately returning with Christ)

Or finally

Amillennialism: (The rejection of a literal rapture of the church)

I know what I believe—But my teaching has always been this:

"That I am on the first load out!" But the timing of the occurrence is not what should be our focus when thinking on the Lord's; it is not how the Lord wants us to occupy our thoughts today.

We who believe and trust on the Lord Jesus Christ know that there is a rumble in the air—a sense that things as we know it are about to change.

Jesus spoke these words in **Mark 13:28-29**

28 "Now learn this parable from the fig tree: When its branch has already become tender, and puts forth leaves, you know that summer is near. 29 So you also, when you see these things happening, know that it is near—at the door!"

As you know, Jesus is talking here about recognizing the signs of the times. Paying attention to the events of the day that herald the fact that the time of Christ return is near; wars, rumors of wars, earthquakes, famines and pestilence. Jesus calls this in **Mark 13:8** *"The beginning of sorrows"* The New International Version (NIV) puts it this way, *"The beginning of birth pains"*—**(NIV)**. Mothers can grasp this analogy very well.

So what do we do with this understanding—Knowing Christ' return is *"At the door"?* Jesus continued farther down in this chapter concerning His return to help us understand how we are to respond—

32 "But of that day and hour no one knows, not even the angels in heaven, nor the Son, but only the Father. 33 Take heed, <u>watch and pray</u>; for you do not know when the time is. 34 It is like a man going to a far country, who left his house and gave authority to his servants, and to each his work, and commanded the doorkeeper to <u>watch</u>. 35 <u>Watch</u> therefore, for you do not know when the master of the house is coming—in the evening, at midnight, at the crowing of the rooster, or in the morning— 36 lest, coming suddenly, he find you sleeping. 37 And what I say to you, I say to all: <u>Watch</u>!"

What Jesus is conveying here is that we need to be ready— watchful!

A couple of years ago I took a break from the office to go home and make lunch for my wife who was going to leave the office as well and meet me there. When I arrived I hurried into the kitchen and began to prepare our sandwiches completely unaware as I past our living room that there was anything out of the ordinary.

After completing the lunch preparation I went into the living room in order to look out the window to see if my wife Kim was pulling into the drive way yet. It was then I noticed the changes in my surroundings. Our flat screen television was missing along with our children's game system. The plants near the items had been knocked over and dirt spilled onto the carpet. Instantly my day changed. A feeling of violation blanketed me; a mix of emotions controlled me—fear, anger, and relief; relief that my wife or children were not home alone when this occurred. But had I known we were going to be broken into I would have been ready—ready with a bat! I would have also warned the neighborhood that there was a potential prowler setting his sights on our homes.

Look what it says in

Ezekiel 33:6-8 (the Lord called Ezekiel a watchman)

⁶ "But if the watchman sees the sword coming and does not blow the trumpet, and the people are not warned, and the sword comes and takes any person from among them, he is taken away in his iniquity; but his blood I will require at the watchman's hand.'
⁷ "So you, son of man: I have made you a watchman for the house of Israel; therefore you shall hear a word from My mouth and <u>warn them</u> for Me. ⁸ When I say to the wicked, 'O wicked man, you shall surely die!' and you do not speak to warn the wicked from his way, that wicked man shall die in his iniquity; but his blood I will require at your hand."

Friends what I hope you are gleaning from these passages is that we need to get busy about the Fathers business by warning others to be ready for the Lord's return—it is imminent! The truth is we have an amazing eternity planned for us with our Lord. Why wouldn't we want to spread the Good News about it that all would have the opportunity to accept Christ and live eternally with Him?

I know that not all will respond to the invitation, but shouldn't we put forth the effort so they cannot say they didn't hear. I do not want to stand before the Lord and him ask me the question—"why didn't you tell others about me?"

And let's also not forget to encourage each other already in the faith—

Remember what **1 Thessalonians 4:18** says, **"Therefore comfort one another with these words."**

Questions to ponder:

1. **What am I witnessing in this world that shows me the time of Christ return is near?**

2. **Who around me is Christ prompting me to give the invitation to accept Him?**

   Additional Scriptural food: Daniel 12:1-3; Matthew 24:41-43; Matthew 25:1-13

Day 28: Christ' Touch is Everything

Do you ever find yourself in a scene like this? Your busy day has come to an end and your family is finally in bed. You shut the lights off and you also crawl in between the sheets with the hope to find sleep as well. Instead you lay there wide eyed staring into the darkness—your mind filled with chaos and uncertainties. In desperation you cry out into what seems like empty space, "Jesus I need your touch!" Even in our emptiness those simple words spoken into the air bring a measure of hope—knowing that on the other end of the line is a receiver whose touch is everything; with a power to resolve our toughest conflict.

We see a scene of desperation like this in a very familiar story in the Word—

In **Matthew 9** Jesus has just passed over by boat back into his home town area. He has also just called Matthew the tax collector to become one of His disciples. Quite a frenzy has already erupted around Him due in part to His hanging around sinners.

We pick up the scene in a house at a table talking with tax collectors and others. The Pharisees who were in the house with Jesus were really having a problem with all that was going on, but things were going to get even more interesting. Look how it reads—

Matthew 9:18-26

18 "While He spoke these things to them, behold, a ruler came and worshiped Him, saying, "My daughter has just died, but come and lay Your hand on her and she will live." 19 So Jesus arose and followed him, and so did His disciples.

20 And suddenly, a woman who had a flow of blood for twelve years came from behind and touched the hem of His garment. 21 For she said to herself, "If only I may touch His garment, I shall be made well." 22 But Jesus turned around, and when He saw her He said, "Be of good cheer, daughter; your faith has made you well." And the woman was made well from that hour. 23 When Jesus came into the ruler's house, and saw the flute players and the noisy crowd wailing, 24 He said to them, "Make room, for the girl is not dead, but sleeping." And they ridiculed Him. 25 But when the crowd was put outside, He went in and took her by the hand, and the girl arose. 26 And the report of this went out into all that land."

In each of these miraculous occurrences there was a touch that took place, and with that touch a transference.

In Luke's Gospel account of the healing of the woman with the issue of blood it records Jesus statement as He turned to see who had touched him.

Luke 8:46, *"But Jesus said, "Somebody touched Me, for I perceived power going out from Me."*

Let's look at another miraculous moment—

Matthew 8:2-4

² And behold, a leper came and worshiped Him, saying, "Lord, if You are willing, You can make me clean." ³ Then Jesus put out His hand and <u>touched him</u>, saying, "I am willing; be cleansed." Immediately his leprosy was cleansed.

These people in their moment of desperate need sought out the <u>source</u> (Jesus). The word Source in the dictionary is defined this way—(the place, person, or thing which something has come into being or from which it has been obtained.)

The Psalmist many times wrote about his source of help in distressing times—

Psalm 40:17 *"But I am poor and needy; yet the Lord thinks upon me. You are <u>my help and my deliverer</u>; do not delay, O my God."*

Once these individuals found the source they needed to plug into it like an outlet in the wall. Let's look at the elements involved in walking in a divine connectivity with Christ

1. **Seek** a strong connection with Jesus
Isaiah 55:6 says, *"<u>Seek the Lord</u> while He may be found, <u>Call upon Him</u> while He is near."*

I have noticed in recent days that the Lord is most interested in our seeking Him. It isn't that Christ isn't there when we call upon His name. What is happening is that Jesus is seeing how we will seek after Him. Our growth and our hunger come with the seeking.

Matthew 5:6 says—

"Blessed are those who hunger and thirst for righteousness, for they shall be filled".

2. After we get plugged into the outlet there will be a **current of power** that goes back and forth. It's that same power that Luke wrote about from Jesus' own words

Luke 8:46, *"...I perceived <u>power going out</u> from Me."*

The fact is you will never receive power unless you are plugged into the source! Try turning on the oven if it is not plugged in and see what happens—nothing!

Once we have the strong connection we need to do the one thing that so many of us have a hard time doing, and that is listening. Oh, we love to talk, but stop and listen, that takes even more effort than most of us want to give.

3. We need to take the time and **be still** and listen.

In this day and age most all of us have a cell phone attached to us any where we go, and depending on where we are can determine whether or not we get a good signal. And many times as we are talking we, and the person on the other end are talking over each other because we are not waiting long enough to actually listen and understand what the person is saying.

Psalm 46:10 says, *"<u>Be still</u>, and know that I am God; I will be exalted among the nations, I will be exalted in the earth!"*

As we read the first few chapters of Revelations, Eight times we see this phrase, *"He who has an ear, let him hear what the Spirit says"*

Hearing, listening, and understanding are keys to responding to the will of the Lord. Ask the Lord today to open your ears and increase your understanding—that you may be able to know Him more.

Question to ponder:

How is my connectivity with Christ?

Additional Scriptural food: Psalm 9:10; Psalm 27:3-5; Psalm 147:5

Day 29: The Great Confession

Matthew 16:13-20

13 "When Jesus came into the region of Caesarea Philippi, He asked His disciples, saying, "Who do men say that I, the Son of Man, am?"

14 So they said, "Some say John the Baptist, some Elijah, and others Jeremiah or one of the prophets."

15 He said to them, "But who do you say that I am?"

16 Simon Peter answered and said, "You are the Christ, the Son of the living God."

17 Jesus answered and said to him, "Blessed are you, Simon Bar-Jonah, for flesh and blood has not revealed this to you, but My Father who is in heaven. 18 And I also say to you that you are Peter, and on this rock I will build My church, and the gates of Hades shall not prevail against it. 19 And I will give you the keys of the kingdom of heaven, and whatever you bind on earth will be bound in heaven, and whatever you loose on earth will be loosed in heaven."

20 Then He commanded His disciples that they should tell no one that He was Jesus the Christ."

At the time of this event in Matthew's Gospel Jesus and His disciples had just left an encounter with the Pharisees and Sadducees. These so called religious and political leaders of the day tried to test Jesus by asking Him to show them a sign. They wanted proof of who He was by theatrics. They had no belief in Him and no faith that He could do the things that were rumored about Him.

But in our text Jesus and His disciples are now in Caesarea Philippi when Jesus turns and ask the big--*"Who do men say that I, the Son of Man, am?"*

Peter heard what others had speculated, but He spent time with Jesus and in His heart it was revealed. The truth just shot out.

"You are the Christ, the Son of the living God."

That Confession of faith filled the atmosphere. All of heaven must have been rejoicing as they heard those words because Peter got it. Jesus declared to Peter and those listening that this understanding hadn't come from man, but God revealed it to him.

Then Jesus spoke these words to his, at times unstable protégé, *"You are Peter!"* Now why did He start it out that way? He had been born **Simon** which in Hebrew simply means *to hear*. So why the sudden name change?

Jesus was declaring into the atmosphere a new era—

Christ said to Simon, *"You are Peter"* which in the Greek is **Petros** which when translated means *a piece of rock.*

Jesus went on to say—*"Upon this Rock"* which uses a different form of the word in the Greek—**Petra** meaning **Massive Rock**.

Peter himself was a little rock, but the confession he spoke was huge, massive, and would have an eternal impact. Christ was going to build His church upon That Great Confession—that *"Jesus is the Son of God."*

It is this confession that sets us apart from all other religions. In fact the apostle John reiterated this fact in his letter in 1 John, it reads—

1 John 4:2-3 (NKJV)

[2] "By this you know the Spirit of God: Every spirit that confesses that Jesus Christ has come in the flesh is of God, [3] and every spirit that does not confess that Jesus Christ has come in the flesh is not of God. And this is the spirit of the Antichrist, which you have heard was coming, and is now already in the world."

And look at what Paul wrote to the church in Rome—

Romans 10:8-10 (NKJV)

[8] "But what does it say? "The word is near you, in your mouth and in your heart" (that is, the word of faith which we preach): [9] that if you confess with your mouth the Lord Jesus and believe in your heart that God has raised Him from the dead, you will be saved. [10] For with the heart one believes unto righteousness, and with the mouth confession is made unto salvation."

Everything we do as a body is built upon the strength of that great confession. We continually minister through the power of that confession.

Looking at the statement "The Lord Jesus" Paul makes in Verse 9 we find that the word Lord in the Greek is **kurios** which means **Supreme authority.** Why am I emphasizing this statement? I believe as Christians we sometimes struggle with the understanding of Christ' supremacy. This is why we walk in defeat so often and not in victory.

Paul said in **1 Corinthians 15:57 (NKJV)**

"But thanks be to God, who gives us the victory through our Lord Jesus Christ."

This is why Jesus turned to His disciples and declared in **Matthew 16:18b** *"...and the gates of Hades <u>will not</u> overcome it (the church)."*

Through this confession of faith the Keys of Heaven were offered to open the gates of the Kingdom to the Jews and Gentiles alike—that they might receive Christ.

Also because of that Great confession we can walk in Victory by binding those things that try to hold us down.

To Bind simply means to forbid, refuse or prohibit.

To Loose means to permit or allow.

Again Jesus said in Matthew 18:18-19

18 "Assuredly, I say to you, whatever you bind on earth will be bound in heaven, and whatever you loose on earth will be loosed in heaven. 19 "Again I say to you that if two of you agree on earth concerning anything that they ask, it will be done for them by My Father in heaven"

Why did Jesus repeat that statement? He wanted it clear the confidence He wants us to walk out our faith in. Walk out your faith today friends with confidence that you are a part of what was built upon that great confession.

Questions to Ponder--

1. What do you forbid, refuse or prohibit?
On the other hand

2. What do you permit or allow?
Additional Scriptural food: Psalm 32:5; Matthew 10:32-33;
Revelation 3:5

Day 30: Becoming a Friend of God

Genesis 15:1-6 (NKJV)

"After these things the word of the Lord came to Abram in a vision, saying, "Do not be afraid, Abram. I am your shield, your exceedingly great reward."

² But Abram said, "Lord God, what will You give me, seeing I go childless, and the heir of my house is Eliezer of Damascus?" ³ Then Abram said, "Look, You have given me no offspring; indeed one born in my house is my heir!"

⁴ And behold, the word of the Lord came to him, saying, "This one shall not be your heir, but one who will come from your own body shall be your heir." ⁵ Then He brought him outside and said, "Look now toward heaven, and count the stars if you are able to number them." And He said to him, "So shall your descendants be."

⁶ And he believed in the Lord, and He accounted it to him for righteousness."

"Becoming A Friend of God"—How does one acquire that privilege as we know Abraham was referred to throughout Scripture?

In the Old and New Testaments we see the prophet Abraham and His unique relationship with God referred too. One such statement is found in the book of 2 Chronicles—

2 Chronicles 20:7 (NKJV)

[7] "Are You not our God, who drove out the inhabitants of this land before Your people Israel, and gave it to the descendants of Abraham Your friend forever?"

And in the New Testament James makes a similar statement—

James 2:23 (NKJV)

[23] "And the Scripture was fulfilled which says, "Abraham believed God, and it was accounted to him for righteousness." And he was called the friend of God."

Why throughout Biblical history was Abraham referred to as "A friend of God"? As we study Scripture we will see that theirs was a relationship that was par none—

Let's take a moment and explore a huge event in their relationship.

We all know the story of Sodom and Gamorah—how the depravity of their sin rose up to God, and the Lord had purposed that He would destroy it from off the face of the earth.

The Angel of the Lord came to Abraham to establish a covenant (*a solemn agreement that is binding on all parties*) with him. God declared that a nation would be built through this covenant.

But as the Angel of the Lord was leaving—He was going toward Sodom to look at its reprobate condition, and then turns back to feel in Abraham on what He is about to do.

We read the account in **Genesis 18:22-29 (NKJV)**

[22] *"Then the men turned away from there and went toward Sodom, but Abraham still stood before the Lord.* [23] *And Abraham came near and said, "Would You also destroy the righteous with the wicked?* [24] *Suppose there were fifty righteous within the city; would You also destroy the place and not spare it for the fifty righteous that were in it?* [25] *Far be it from You to do such a thing as this, to slay the righteous with the wicked, so that the righteous should be as the wicked; far be it from You! Shall not the Judge of all the earth do right?"*

[26] *So the Lord said, "If I find in Sodom fifty righteous within the city, then I will spare all the place for their sakes."*

[27] *Then Abraham answered and said, "Indeed now, I who am but dust and ashes have taken it upon myself to speak to the Lord:* [28] *Suppose there were five less than the fifty righteous; would You destroy all of the city for lack of five?"*

So He said, "If I find there forty-five, I will not destroy it."

²⁹ And he spoke to Him yet again and said, "Suppose there should be forty found there?"

So He said, "I will not do it for the sake of forty."

³⁰ Then he said, "Let not the Lord be angry, and I will speak: Suppose thirty should be found there?"

So He said, "I will not do it if I find thirty there."

³¹ And he said, "Indeed now, I have taken it upon myself to speak to the Lord: Suppose twenty should be found there?"

So He said, "I will not destroy it for the sake of twenty."

³² Then he said, "Let not the Lord be angry, and I will speak but once more: Suppose ten should be found there?"

And He said, "I will not destroy it for the sake of ten." ³³ So the Lord went His way as soon as He had finished speaking with Abraham; and Abraham returned to his place."

There was a reasoning going on between the Lord and Abraham. Abraham could stand before God and voice his concerns—empty His heart out to try and move the hand of the Lord. And because of that relationship and the fact that The Lord new Abraham believed what the Lord had told him, in what we call the "Abrahamic covenant", God responded in heading the cry of Abraham's heart.

The apostle Paul made reference to this Genesis quote in **Romans 4:3,** *"For what does the Scripture say? "Abraham believed God, and it was accounted to him for righteousness."*

The word account in both the Greek and the Hebrew is the same word for *"Impute"* (to extend a quality to somebody else) God had placed this mantle upon him because of his faith.

As I began to think about this "Friend of God idea" I thought of a moment I had with the Lord and a conversation that ensue about it in a cohort I lead at work.

In this meeting I shared about this personal moment I had with the Lord in the middle of the night. My head was full of task that needed to be accomplished and the insecurities I felt in being able to accomplish them. I felt very inadequate. I looked up toward heaven and exclaimed, "Lord, I can't do this!"

When I asked those in the group if they could relate to what I was talking about a spattering of Christian rhetoric was thrown around—"Greater is He that is in me than He that is in the world" and "I can do all things through Christ that strengthens me."

The truth is I believe all of that for it is straight out of God's word, but we can also be real and speak with the Lord how we feel. We don't need to hide behind a mask of always having it spiritually together.

What occurred to me in that meeting was that the statement I made to the Lord was true—I can't do it, But Christ can, and He knows my heart or insecurities and as a friend of God He will carry it.

So again I emphasize this question—how can one become "A friend of God"?

Look at Jesus' own words in—

John 15:13-15 (NKJV)

[13] "Greater love has no one than this, than to lay down one's life for his friends. [14] You are My friends if you do whatever I command you. [15] No longer do I call you servants, for a servant does not know what his master is doing; but I have called you friends, for all things that I heard from My Father I have made known to you."

It's all about obedience—Doing what Christ says and believing His Word.

Why was Abraham a friend of God? Because He believed God—Pure and simple!

Questions to ponder:

1. How would I describe my relationship with God?

2. Do I trust the Lord to fulfill His purpose for my life?

    Additional Scriptural food: Psalm 77; Psalm 4:4-6;
    Psalm 9:9-11; Nahum 1:7; 1Timothy 4:10

Day 31: Remember This

Lamentations 3:1-26 (NKJV)

"I am the man who has seen affliction by the rod of His wrath.
² He has led me and made me walk in darkness and not in light.
³ Surely He has turned His hand against me time and time again
throughout the day. ⁴ He has aged my flesh and my skin, and
broken my bones. ⁵ He has besieged me and surrounded me with
bitterness and woe. ⁶ He has set me in dark places like the dead of
long ago. ⁷ He has hedged me in so that I cannot get out; He has
made my chain heavy. ⁸ Even when I cry and shout, He shuts out
my prayer. ⁹ He has blocked my ways with hewn stone; He has
made my paths crooked. ¹⁰ He has been to me a bear lying in wait,
like a lion in ambush. ¹¹ He has turned aside my ways and torn me
in pieces; He has made me desolate. ¹² He has bent His bow and
set me up as a target for the arrow.

¹³ He has caused the arrows of His quiver to pierce my loins. ¹⁴ I
have become the ridicule of all my people—their taunting song all
the day. ¹⁵ He has filled me with bitterness, He has made me drink
wormwood. ¹⁶ He has also broken my teeth with gravel, and
covered me with ashes. ¹⁷ You have moved my soul far from peace;
I have forgotten prosperity. ¹⁸ And I said, "My strength and my
hope have perished from the Lord." ¹⁹ Remember my affliction
and roaming, the wormwood and the gall. ²⁰ My soul still

remembers and sinks within me. ²¹ This I recall to my mind,
therefore I have hope. ²² Through the Lord's mercies we are not
consumed, because His compassions fail not. ²³ They are new
every morning; great is Your faithfulness. ²⁴ "The Lord is my
portion," says my soul, "Therefore I hope in Him!"
²⁵ The Lord is good to those who wait for Him, to the
soul who seeks Him.
²⁶ It is good that one should hope and wait quietly for the salvation
of the Lord."

When we begin reading this chapter it is not very
encouraging. In fact just the first few verses make you glad you are
not Jeremiah in the overwhelming time he is having. But as we read
on most of us can relate to the day he is describing. If we are honest
many passages like this are not ones we want to spend much time in.
We would probably be tempted to stopped reading after just a few
verses in.

Forcing ourselves to trudge along in this passage we would
notice that in **Verse 20** Jeremiah makes a paradigm shift—**"This I
recall to my mind, therefore I have hope."** Jeremiah's mind starts
to go someplace different. Even in the middle of his pain He
remembers the Lord's faithfulness.

As I began to journey through this passage and all that
Jeremiah was going through something ironic occurred. Pain began
to rack my body—my upper and lower back began to hurt. It caused

me great distraction. Did I happen to mention my knee was hurting too?

I could feel a whine coming on!

Two options were suddenly presented to me—quickly change the topic of study or try to relate to it. I chose the latter of the two. As simplistic and minute my ailments were in compared to the physical manifestations Jeremiah was experiencing as a result of the grief for Israel I knew I must use my pain as a way to relate, and I hope, as you study this story, will use whatever you are going through, to try to relate to what Jeremiah is lamenting here.

If we are truly going to relate we must put ourselves in the mindset and heart of the prophet Jeremiah. Jeremiah's eyes were not on his personal plight, but rather upon the condition of his nation's heart and the consequences resulting from their rebellion toward God.

God's lack of response was due to Israel's sin. Jeremiah knew that, but prayed and wept anyway calling on God for his nation, and in his lament he is reminded of God's character.

Jeremiahs first shift of thought goes to The Lord's mercy. No matter the bleak situation, he knew that the reason they were not destroyed is according to—

Verse 22-23, "*Through* the <u>Lord's mercies</u> we are not consumed, Because His compassions fail not. [23] *They are* new every

morning;

Great *is* Your faithfulness."

Let's look at three of the character traits of the Lord that Jeremiah emphasizes—

1. Mercy

Jeremiah stated that because of the Lord's mercy they will not be consumed, or destroyed even though he knew they deserved it. The Hebrew word for mercy the prophet uses here is Chacad-- *khawsad*. This Hebrew word used about 250 times in the Old Testament, refers to God's gracious love. It is a comprehensive term that encompasses love, grace, mercy, goodness, forgiveness, truth, compassion, and faithfulness.

The Psalmist in Psalm 13 had the same reflection as Jeremiah, moving from reflecting on the harsh situation to the mercies of the Lord. **Psalm 13 (NKJV)** says,

"How long, O Lord? Will You forget me forever?

How long will You hide Your face from me?

² How long shall I take counsel in my soul,

Having sorrow in my heart daily?

How long will my enemy be exalted over me?

³ Consider _and_ hear me, O Lord my God;

Enlighten my eyes,

Lest I sleep the _sleep of_ death;

⁴ Lest my enemy say,

"I have prevailed against him";

Lest those who trouble me rejoice when I am moved.

⁵ But I have trusted in Your mercy;

My heart shall rejoice in Your salvation.

⁶ I will sing to the Lord,

Because He has dealt bountifully with me."

2. Compassion *"His compassions fail not—they are new every morning"*

What an amazing truth this is that each morning we wake the Lord's compassions are there—fresh and new. It doesn't grow stale or run out. Again in the writings of the Psalmist we see a similar sentiment.

Psalm 78:37-39 (NKJV)

"For their heart was not steadfast with Him,

Nor were they faithful in His covenant.

But He, being full of compassion, forgave their iniquity,

And did not destroy them.

Yes, many a time He turned His anger away,

And did not stir up all His wrath;

For He remembered that they were but flesh,

A breath that passes away and does not come again."

3.   Faithfulness

Jeremiah says God's faithfulness is great—not average or shallow, nor is it something to be unsure of. It is faithfulness beyond human comprehension.

So often we run into people who have been hurt by a lack of faithfulness by someone they were close too. Perhaps you have been the one whose faithfulness was less than great.

Whatever the scenario many of us have had our trust challenged, but with Christ we never have to wonder. He will always be faithful. The question we need to ask ourselves is will I remain faithful to Him?

The Apostle Paul wrote these words to the church in Rome in—
Romans 3:1-4 (NKJV)

> *"What advantage then has the Jew, or what is the profit of circumcision? Much in every way! Chiefly because to them were committed the oracles of God. 3 For what if some did not believe? Will their unbelief make the faithfulness of God without effect? 4 Certainly not! Indeed, let God be true but every man a liar. As it is written:*
> *"That You may be justified in Your words, and may overcome when You are judged."*

The truth is that even when we are faithless God is faithful! The bedrock of faith is the reality that God keeps all His promises according to His truthful faithful Character.

No matter the pain and torment or the condition of our world and what we see happening around us God is faithful, God is compassionate, and God is merciful. Let us cry out to the God of mercy, faithfulness, and compassion, as Jeremiah did, for the restoration of our nation, our neighbor, and our own condition.

Questions to ponder:

1. **How have you seen the Lord's faithfulness shine through in the dark times of your life?**

2. **How have you seen the Lord use the shattered moments of your life?**

   Additional Scriptural food: Psalm 25:7; Psalm 86:15; Psalm 119:90; Titus 3:1-7